June Jordan

ON CALL

Political Essays

South End Press   Boston, MA

Cover photo: June Jordan with Francisco Campbell in an area of Teotecacinte that had recently been bombed by the contras.

Cover photo by Jonathan Snow
Cover design by Cynthia Peters

Jordan, June 1936-
On Call
I Title.
PS 3560.07305   1985   909.82'8
ISBN 0-89608-268-7
ISBN 0-89608-269-5 (pbk)

South End Press   116 Saint Botolph St.   Boston, MA   02115

Note

Given that they were first to exist on the planet and currently make up the majority, the author will refer to that part of the population usually termed Third World as the First World.

Essays that were previously published are listed below:

"For the Sake of A People's Poetry" first appeared as the introductory essay to my book of poems, entitled *Passion*, published by Beacon Press in 1980. This essay was subsequently anthologized in *Walt Whitman: The Measure of His Song,* edited by Perlman, Folsom, Campion and published by Holy Cow! Press, 1981. "South Africa: Bringing it All Back Home" was published in *The New York Times"* on September 26, 1981. "Many Rivers to Cross" was first presented as the keynote address for the conference on "Women and Work," December 11, 1981 at Barnard College. Subsequently, it was published in *Savvy,* July, 1982. "Problems of Language in a Democratic State" was presented as the keynote address to the National Conference of the Teachers of English annual conference, in Washington D.C., 1982. "The Case for the Real Majority" was published by the Boston Globe in June, 1982. "Report from the Bahamas" was originally presented as a keynote address to the New England Women's Studies Association Conference, Salem, Mass, 1982. It appeared later in *Ms.* magazine, November, 1982. "Love is Not the Problem" was published in *Dial* magazine, February, 1983. "Black Folks on Nicaragua: 'Leave Those Folks Alone!'" published in the October 4, 1983 issue of *The Village Voice.* "Nicaragua: Why I had to go There" was originally published in the January, 1984 issue of *Essence.* "Life After Lebanon" was first presented in October, 1984 as a keynote address to the Mid-Atlantic Women's Studies Association Conference. It subsequently appeared in *Sojourner,* June, 1985. "The Miracle of Black Poetry: Or something Like a Sonnet for Phillis Wheatley" was the keynote address for the Bi-Centennial Celebration of Phillis Wheatley at the University of Massachusetts, Amherst, February 4, 1985. "Black People and the Law: A Tribute to William Kunstler" was presented March 1, 1985 as an introduction to William Kunstler, Esq. on the occasion of his being honored by the New York Lawyers Guild. "In Our Hands" was published by *Essence* in May, 1985. "The Blood Shall Be A Sign Unto You: Israel and South Africa" was presented at the Foreign Policy Panel of the Socialist Scholars Conference in New York City, April 6, 1985. "Columbia University Students' Protest Against Apartheid" was an address to the students who sat in at the administration building of Columbia University for two weeks in April. "White Tuesday" was published in *The Village Voice* on November 20, 1984.

Dedicated to:
The Future Life of Willie Jordan

Table of Contents

Introduction

I am very pleased by the publication of this second set of my political writings. Several of these essays have been published, previously, in national magazines. But many of them have not. Perhaps you will find it instructive to notice the have-nots. Certainly I do: I am learning, first hand, about American censorship.

In a sense, this book must compensate for the absence of a cheaper and more immediate, print outlet for my two cents. If political writing by a Black woman did not strike so many editors as presumptuous or simply bizarre then, perhaps, this book would not be needed. Instead, I might regularly appear, on a weekly or monthly schedule, as a national columnist. But if you will count the number of Black women with regular and national forums for their political ideas, and the ideas of their constituency, you will comprehend the politics of our exclusion: I cannot come up with the name of *one* Black woman in that position.

Beyond the denial of print to Black women, there is the fact of silence imposed upon all Black people. For example, today is August 30, 1985. The South African "State of Emergency" has been in effect now for more than a month. During this period, the *New York Times* has published not a single op-ed on the subject of South Africa by any Afro-American writer in this country: Not one. The fact of our absence, the fact that the *Times* has obviously not sought *many* Black points of view on this issue is amazing. Black people do not appear in mass media on subjects of crucial meaning to us because media institutions systematically dare to interdict our right and our need to pose our views in the realm of public debate.

1

I am learning about American censorship.

On the left, as well as in the mainstream, airborne orthodoxies attempt to identify the correct subject matters for discussion, as well as the correct points of view. There are "correct" or "suitable" subjects for women to contemplate. A leading women's magazine rejected my essay on Walt Whitman and New World Literature, explaining that it was neither "appropriate" for their readers, nor acceptably "feminist." This same magazine later published an essay of mine on race and class in their "travel and leisure" section! For Black people, there are also "incorrect" or "inappropriate" subjects to engage. Foreign and nuclear policies or the trees of our environment used to be strictly "white" issues presumably irrelevant to most Black folks. And then there are always sudden limits to permissible points of view. For instance, the mainstream often will not allow anyone to write in support of certain countries, or regimes that the left will not permit anyone to criticize. And for all of the mainstream and most of the left, freedoms of speech and of the press remain questions that basically apply only to faraway writers who would require a visa just to appear among us.

Here, supposedly, we do not have "dissident" poets and writers—unless they are well rewarded runaways from the Soviet Union. Here we know about the poets and writers that major media eagerly allow us to see and consume. And then we do not hear about the other ones. But I am one of them. I am a dissident American poet and writer completely uninterested to run away from my country, my home.

Because my politics devolve from my entire real life, and real phone calls and meetings about real horror or triumph happening to other real people, none of it respects or reflects any orthodox anything, any artifice of position or concern. From Phillis Wheatley to Walt Whitman, from Stony Brook to Lebanon, these writings document my political efforts to coherently fathom all of my universe, and to arrive at a moral judgement that will determine my further political conduct. Except for the opening essay, "For the Sake of a People's Poetry," written in 1979, this collection brings together the political writings that the past four years have caused me to produce. During this time, more and more varieties of American people have invited me to speak to them. From the Columbia University Students' protest against apartheid to the National Conference of the Teachers of English, I have been honored, increasingly, by nationwide opportunities to share my political experience and ideas with strangers who frequently become my friends—whether or not we agree with each other.

Simultaneously, I have encountered new and considerable resistance to the publication of my work. In this way, I have been whitelisted by editors who have plainly enough written or said to me: "We love your writing but too many of us have problems with your position on Nicaragua. Or the Middle East." They don't say "We don't agree with you and so we will not publish your work." They don't say, "We don't believe you have a right to any opinion on this matter." These editors hide behind "many of us" who "have problems" with me. Apparently, there is some magisterial and unnameable "we" who decided—in the cowardly passive voice—what "is punishable" or not. I need to know who is this "we," exactly? And what are "the problems"?

I am learning about American censorship.

And I am gaining important connections to people who are actually not so different as American censorship might have you believe. For example, I am indebted to the Israeli writer, Benjamin Beit Hallahmi, an editor of the Israeli publication, *New Outlook* and Professor of Psychology at the University of Haifa, for his decidedly generous help with the research for my essay, "The Blood Shall Be A Sign Unto You." I am cheered, and instructed by the interview that the Israeli journalist, Yo'Av Karny, chose to conduct and then publish as a feature article presenting my views in *Ha'aretz,* earlier this year.

I am honored by this opportunity and by my need to say thank you, with much love to the novelist, playwright, critic and poet, Mr. Wesley Brown.

It is also my privilege to express my gratitude to Susan Taylor and Cheryll Greene of *Essence* magazine, to Jean Carey Bond of *Freedomways,* to Attorney Gay McDougall, Director of the Southern Africa Project of the Lawyers Committee for Civil Rights Under Law, to the poet, Thulani Davis, who was Senior Editor at *The Village Voice,* until recently, to my students at Stony Brook, to John Bracey and Ernie Allen of the W.E.B. DuBois Department of Afro-American Studies at the University of Massachusetts at Amherst, to Barabara Christian, Chair of the Department of Afro-American Studies at the University of California at Berkeley, to Carolyn Porter, to Arlene Avakian, to Lisa Baskin, to Michael Ratner, to Sara, to Christopher, to Richard, to Alice, to Zaki, and absolutely, to Adrienne.

And a final thank you to Jade Barker and to my editor, Cynthia Peters, and to the South End Press collective. Here it really is, *On Call:*

Chapter 1

For the Sake of People's Poetry
Walt Whitman and the Rest of Us
1981

In America, the father is white; it is he who inaugurated the experiment of this republic. It is he who sailed his way into slave ownership and who availed himself of my mother—that African woman whose function was miserable—defined by his desirings, or his rage. It is he who continues to dominate the destiny of the Mississippi River, the Blue Ridge Mountains, and the life of my son. Understandably, then, I am curious about this man.

Most of the time my interest can be characterized as wary, at best. Other times, it is the interest a pedestrian feels for the fast traveling truck about to smash into him. Or her. Again. And at other times it is the curiosity of a stranger trying to figure out the system of the language that excludes her name and all of the names of all of her people. It is this last that leads me to the poet Walt Whitman.

Trying to understand the system responsible for every boring, inaccessible, irrelevant, derivative and pretentious poem that is glued to the marrow of required readings in American classrooms, or trying to understand the system responsible for the exclusion of every hilarious, amazing, visionary, pertinent and unforgettable poet from National Endowment of the Arts grants and from national publications, I come back to Walt Whitman.

What in the hell happened to him? Wasn't he a white man? Wasn't he some kind of a father to American literature? Didn't he talk about this New World? Didn't he see it? Didn't he sing this New World, this America, on a New World, an American scale of his own visionary invention?

5

It so happens that Walt Whitman is the one white father who share the systematic disadvantages of his heterogeneous off- spring trapped inside a closet that is, in reality, as huge as the continental spread of North and South America. What Whitman envisioned, we, the people and the poets of the New World, embody. He has been punished for the moral questions that our very lives arouse.

At home as a child, I learned the poetry of the Bible and the poetry of Paul Laurence Dunbar. As a student, I diligently fol- lowed orthodox directions from *The Canterbury Tales* right through *The Wasteland* by that consummate Anglophile whose name I can never remember. And I kept waiting. It was, I thought, all right to deal with daffodils in the 17th century of an island as much like Manhattan as I resemble Queen Mary. But what about Dunbar? When was he coming up again? And where were the Black poets, altogether? And who were the women poets I might reasonably emulate? And wasn't there, ever, a great poet who was crazy about Brooklyn or furious about war? And I kept waiting. And I kept writing my own poetry. And I kept reading apparently underground poetry: poetry kept strictly off campus. I kept read- ing the poetry of so many gifted students when I became a teacher. I kept listening to the wonderful poetry of the multiplying numbers of my friends who were and who are New World poets until I knew, for a fact, that there was and that there is an Ameri- can, a New World poetry that is as personal, as public, as irresisti- ble, as quick, as necessary, as unprecedented, as representative, as exalted, as speakably commonplace, and as musical as an emer- gency phone call.

But I didn't know about Walt Whitman. Yes, I had heard about this bohemian, this homosexual, even, who wrote something about The Captain and The Lilacs in The Hallway, but nobody ever told me to read his work! Not only was Whitman not required reading, he was, on the contrary, presented as a rather hairy buffoon suffering from a childish proclivity for exercise and open air.

Nevertheless, it is through the study of the poems and the ideas of this particular white father that I have reached a tactical, if not strategic, understanding of the racist, sexist, and anti- American predicament that condemns most New World writing to peripheral/unpublished manuscript status.

Before these United States came into being, the great poets of the world earned their lustre through undeniable forms of spontaneous popularity; generations of a people chose to memorize and then to further elaborate these songs and to impart them to the next generation. I am talking about people; African families and Greek families and the families of the Hebrew tribes and all that multitude to whom the Bhagavad-Gita is as daily as the sun! If these poems were not always religious, they were certainly moral in notice, or in accomplishment, or both. None of these great poems would be mistaken for the poetry of another country, another time. You do not find a single helicopter taking off or landing in any of the sonnets of Elizabethan England, nor do you run across rice and peas in any of the psalms! Evidently, one criterion for great poetry used to be the requirements of cultural nationalism.

But by the advent of the thirty-six year old poet, Walt Whitman, the phenomenon of a people's poetry, or great poetry and its spontaneous popularity, could no longer be assumed. The physical immensity and the farflung population of this New World decisively separated poets from suitable means to produce and distribute their poetry. Now there would have to be intermediaries—critics and publishers—whose marketplace principles of scarcity would, logically, oppose them to populist traditions of art.

Old World concepts would replace the democratic and these elitist notions would prevail; in the context of such considerations, an American literary establishment antithetical to the New World meanings of America took root. And this is one reason why the pre-eminently American white father of American poetry exists primarily in the realm of caricature and rumor in his own country.

As a matter of fact, if you hope to hear about Whitman your best bet is to leave home. Ignore prevailing American criticism and, instead, ask anybody anywhere else in the world this question: As Shakespeare is to England, Dante to Italy, Tolstoy to Russia, Goethe to Germany, Aghostino Neto to Angola, Pablo Neruda to Chile, Mao-Tse-Tung to China, and Ho Chi Minh to Vietnam, who is the great American writer, the distinctively American poet, the giant American "literatus"? Undoubtedly, the answer will be *Walt Whitman*.

He is the poet who wrote:

"A man's body at auction
(For before the war I often go to the slave-mart and watch the sale.)

> I help the auctioneer, the sloven does not half know his
> business...
> Gentlemen look on this wonder.
> Whatever the bids of the bidders they cannot be high
>   enough for it [1]

I ask you, today: Who in the United States would publish those lines? They are all wrong! In the first place there is nothing obscure, nothing contrived, nothing an ordinary strap-hanger in the subway would be puzzled by! In the second place, the voice of those lines is intimate and direct, at once; it is the voice of the poet who assumes that he speaks to an equal and that he need not fear that equality. On the contrary, the intimate distance between the poet and the reader is a distance that assumes there is everything important, between them, to be shared. And what is poetic about a line of words that runs as long as a regular, a spoken idea? You could more easily imagine an actual human being speaking such lines than you could imagine an artist composing them in a room carefully separated from the real life of his family. This can't be poetry! Besides, these lines apparently serve an expressly moral purpose! Then is this didactic/political writing? Aha! This cannot be *good* poetry. And, in fact, you will never see, for example, *The New Yorker* Magazine publishing a poem marked by such splendid deficiencies.

Consider the inevitable, the irresistible, simplicity of that enormous moral idea:

> Gentlemen look on this wonder.
> Whatever the bids of the bidders they cannot be high
>   enough for it...
> This is not only one man, this the father of those who
>   shall be fathers in their turns
> In him the start of populous states and rich republics, Of
>   him countless immortal lives with countless embodi-
>   ments and enjoyments

Crucial and obviously important and, hence, this is not an idea generally broadcast: the poet is trying to save a human being while even the *poem* cannot be saved from the insolence of marketplace evaluation!

Indeed Whitman and the traceable descendants of Walt Whitman, those who follow his democratic faith into obviously New World forms of experience and art, they suffer from establishment rejection and contempt the same as forced this archety-

pal American genius to publish, distribute, and review his own
work, by himself. The descendants I have in mind include those
unmistakeably contemporaneous young poets who base themselves upon domesticities such as disco, Las Vegas, MacDonalds,
and $40 running shoes. Also within the Whitman tradition, Black
and First World* poets traceably transform and further the egalitarian sensibility that isolates that one white father from his more
powerful compatriots. I am thinking of the feminist poets evidently intent upon speaking with a maximal number and diversity of other Americans lives. I am thinking of all the many first
rank heroes of the New World who are overwhelmingly forced to
publish their own works using a hand press, or whatever, or else
give it up entirely.

That is to say, the only peoples who can test or verify the
meaning of the United States as a democratic state, as a pluralistic
culture, these are the very peoples whose contribution to a national
vision and discovery meet with steadfast ridicule and disregard.

A democratic state does not, after all, exist for the few, but for
the many. A democratic state is not proven by the welfare of the
strong but by the welfare of the weak. And unless that many, that
manifold constitution of diverse peoples can be seen as integral to
the national art/the national consciousness, you might as well
mean only Czechoslovakia when you talk about the USA, or only
Ireland, or merely France, or exclusively white men.

Pablo Neruda is a New World poet whose fate differs from the
other Whitman descendants because he was born into a country
where the majority of the citizens did not mistake themselves for
Englishmen or long to find themselves struggling, at most, with
cucumber sandwiches and tea. He was never European. His
anguish was not aroused by three piece suits and rolled umbrellas.
When he cries, towards the conclusion of *The Heights of Macchu
Picchu,* "Arise and birth with me, my brother,"[2] he plainly does not
allude to Lord or Colonel Anybody At All. As he writes earlier, in
that amazing poem:

> I came by another way, river by river, street after street,
> city by city, one bed and another,
> forcing the salt of my mask through a wilderness;
> and there, in the shame of the ultimate hovels, lampless
> and tireless,
> lacking bread or a stone or a stillness, alone in myself,
> I whirled at my will, dying the death that was mine[3]

*See *Note* on page iv.

Of course Neruda has not escaped all of the untoward consequences common to Whitman descendants. American critics and trans-
lators never weary of asserting that Neruda is a quote great
unquote poet *despite* the political commitment of his art and despite the artistic consequences of the commitment. Specifically,
Neruda's self-conscious decision to write in a manner readily comprehensible to the masses of his countrymen, and his self-
conscious decision to specify, outright, the United Fruit Company
when that was the instigating subject of his poem, become unfortunate moments in an otherwise supposedly sublime, not to mention surrealist, deeply Old World and European but nonetheless
Chilean case history. To assure the validity of this perspective, the
usual American critic and translator presents you with a smatter-
ing of the unfortunate, ostensibly political poetry and, on the other
hand, buries you under volumes of Neruda's early work that antedates the Spanish Civil War or, in other words, that antedates
Neruda's serious conversion to a political world view.

This kind of artistically indefensible censorship would have
you perceive qualitative and even irreconcilable differences between the poet who wrote:

You, my antagonist, in that splintering dream
like the bristling glass of gardens, like a menace of rui-
nous bells, volleys
of blackening ivy at the perfume's center,
enemy of the great hipbones my skin has touched
with a harrowing dew[4]

And the poet who wrote, some twenty years later, these lines from
the poem entitled *The Dictators*:

Lament was perpetual and fell, like a plant and its
pollen,
forcing a lightless increase in the blinded, big leaves
And bludgeon by bludgeon, on the terrible waters,
scale over scale in the bog,
the snout filled with silence and slime
and vendetta was born[5]

According to prevalent American criticism, that later poem of
Neruda represents a lesser achievement precisely because it can be
understood by more people, more easily, than the first. It is also
derogated because this poem attacks a keystone of the Old World,

namely dictatorship or, in other words, power and privilege for the few.

The peculiar North American vendetta against Walt Whit-man, against the first son of this democratic union, can be further fathomed if you look at some facts: Neruda's eminence is now acknowledged on international levels; it is known to encompass profound impact upon North American poets who do not realize the North American/Walt Whitman origins for so much that is singular and worthy in the poetry of Neruda. You will even find American critics who congratulate Neruda for overcoming the "Whitmanesque" content of his art. This perfidious arrogance is as calculated as it is common. You cannot persuade anyone seriously familiar with Neruda's life and art that he could have found cause, at any point, to disagree with the tenets, the analysis and the authentic New World vision presented by Walt Whitman in his essay, *Democratic Vistas,* which remains the most signal and persuasive manifesto of New World thinking and belief in print.

Let me define my terms, in brief: New World does not mean New England. New World means non-European; it means new; it means big; it means heterogenous; it means unknown; it means free; it means an end to feudalism, caste, privilege, and the vio-lence of power. It means *wild* in the sense that a tree growing away from the earth enacts a wild event. It means *democratic* in the sense that, as Whitman wrote:

> I believe a leaf of grass is no less than
> the journey-work of the stars...
> And a mouse is miracle enough to stagger
> sextillions of infidels[6]

New World means that, as Whitman wrote, "I keep as delicate around the bowels as around the head and heart." New World means, as Whitman said, "By God! I will accept nothing which all cannot have their counterpart of on the same terms."

In *Democratic Vistas,* Whitman declared,

> As the greatest lessons of Nature through the universe
> are perhaps the lessons of variety and freedom, the same
> present the greatest lessons also in New World politics
> and progress...Sole among nationalities, these States
> have assumed the task to put in forms of history, power

and practicality, on areas of amplitude rivaling the oper-
ations of the physical kosmos, the moral political specu-
lations of ages, long, long deffer'd, the democratic republican principle, and the theory of development and perfec-
tion by voluntary standards and self reliance.

Listen to this white father; he is so weird! Here he is calling aloud
for an American, a democratic spirit. An American, a democratic
idea that could morally constrain and coordinate the material
body of USA affluence and piratical outreach, more than a
hundred years ago he wrote,

The great poems, Shakespeare included, are poisonous to
the idea of the pride and dignity of the common people,
the lifeblood of democracy. The models of our literature,
as we get it from other lands, ultra marine, have had their
birth in courts, and bask'd and grown in castle sunshine;
all smells of princes' favors...Do you call those genteel
little creatures American poets? Do you term that perpetual, pistareen, paste-pot work, American art, American
drama, taste, verse?...We see the sons and daughters of
The New World, ignorant of its genius, not yet inaugurat-
ing the native, the universal, and the near, still importing
the distant, the partial, the dead.

Abhorring the "thin sentiment of parlors, parasols, piano-song,
tinkling rhymes," Whitman conjured up a poetry of America, a
poetry of democracy which would not "mean the smooth walks,
trimm'd hedges, poseys and nightingales of the English poets, but
the whole orb, with its geologic history, the Kosmos, carrying fire
and snow that rolls through the illimitable areas, light as a
feather, though weighing billions of tons."

Well, what happened?

Whitman went ahead and wrote the poetry demanded by his
vision. He became, by thousands upon thousands of words, a great
American poet:

There was a child went forth every day,
And the first object he look'd upon, that object he became,
And that object became part of him for the day
Or a certain part of the day,
Or for many years or stretching cycles of years
The early lilacs became part of this child,
And grass and white and red morning-glories,

and white and red clover, and the song of the phoebe-
bird...[7]

And, elsewhere, he wrote:

> It avails not, time nor place—distance avails not,
> I am with you, you men and women of a generation,
> or ever some many generations hence,
> Just as you feel when you look on the river and sky,
> so I felt,
> Just as any of you is one of a living crowd, I was one of a
> crowd,
> Just as you are refresh'd by the gladness of the river
> and the bright flow, I was refresh'd,
> Just as you stand and lean on the rail, yet
> hurry with the swift current, I stood yet was hurried,
> Just as you look on the numberless masts of ships and the
> thick-stemm'd pipes of steamboats,
> I look'd...[8]

This great American poet of democracy as cosmos, this poet of a
continent as consciousness, this poet of the many people as one
people, this poet of diction comprehensible to all, of a vision insist-
ing on each, of a rhythm/a rhetorical momentum to transport the
reader from the Brooklyn ferry into the hills of Alabama and back
again, of line after line of bodily, concrete detail that constitutes
the mysterious the cellular tissue of a nation indivisible but
dependent upon and astonishing in its diversity, this white father
of a great poetry deprived of its spontaneous popularity/a great
poetry hidden away from the ordinary people it celebrates so well,
he has been, again and again, cast aside as an undisciplined
poseur, a merely freak eruption of prolix perversities.

Last year, the *New York Times Book Review* saw fit to import
a European self-appointed critic of American literature to address
the question: Is there a great American poet? Since this visitor was
ignorant of the philosophy and the achievements of Walt Whitman, the visitor, Denis Donoghue, comfortably excluded every
possible descendent of Whitman from his erstwhile cerebrations.
Only one woman was mentioned (she, needless to add, did not
qualify). No poets under fifty, and not one Black or First World
poet received even cursory assessment. Not one poet of distinctively New World values, and their formal embodiment, managed
to dent the suavity of Donoghue's public display.

This *New York Times* event perpetuated American habits of beggarly, absurd deference to the Old World. And these habits bespeak more than marketplace intrusions into cultural realms. We erase ourselves through self hatred. We lend our silence to the American anti-American process whereby anything and anyone special to this nation state becomes liable to condemnation because it is what it is, truly.

Against self hatred there is Whitman and there are all of the New World poets who insistently devise legitimate varieties of cultural nationalism. There is Whitman and all of the poets whose lives have been baptized by witness to blood, by witness to cataclysmic, political confrontations from the Civil War through the Civil Rights Era, through the Women's Movement, and on and on through the conflicts between the hungry and the well-fed, the wasteful, the bullies.

In the poetry of the New World, you meet with a reverence for the material world that begins with a reverence for human life. There is an intellectual trust in sensuality as a means of knowledge, an easily deciphered system of reference, aspirations to a believable, collective voice and, consequently, emphatic preference for broadly accessible, spoken language. Deliberately balancing perception with vision, it seeks to match moral exhortation with sensory report.

All of the traceable descendants of Whitman have met with an establishment, academic reception disgracefully identical; except for the New World poets who live and write beyond the boundaries of the USA, the offspring of this one white father encounter everlasting marketplace disparagement as crude or optional or simplistic or, as Whitman himself wrote "hankering, gross, mystical, nude."

I too am a descendant of Walt Whitman. And I am not by myself stuggling to tell the truth about this history of so much land and so much blood, of so much that should be sacred and so much that has been desecrated and annihilated boastfully.

My brothers and my sisters of this New World, we remember that, as Whitman said,

> I do not trouble my spirit to vindicate
> itself or be understood,
> I see that the elementary laws never **apologize**[9]

We do not apologize that we are not Emily Dickinson, Ezra Pound, T.S. Eliot, Wallace Stevens, Robert Lowell, and Elizabeth Bishop.

Or, as Whitman exclaimed, "I exist as I am, that is enough."

New World poetry moves into and beyond the light of the lives of Walt Whitman, Pablo Neruda, Aghostino Neto, Gabriela Mistral, Langston Hughes, and Margaret Walker. I follow this movement with my own life. I am calm and I am smiling as we go. Is it not written, somewhere very near to me:

> A man's body at auction...
> Gentlemen, look on this wonder,
> Whatever the bids of the bidders,
> They cannot be high enough for it...

And didn't that weird white father predict this truth that is always growing:

> I swear to you the architects shall appear without fail,
> I swear to you they will understand you and justify you
> The greatest among them shall be he who best knows you
> and encloses all and is faithful to all,
> He and the rest shall not forget you, they shall
> perceive that you are not an iota less than they,
> You shall be fully glorified in them[10]

Walt Whitman and all of the New World poets coming after him, we, too, go on singing this America.

Chapter 2

South Africa:
Bringing it All Back Home
September, 1981

I used to imagine South Africa somewhere hidden as deep as the most unspeakable fears that I knew as a child. I used to think it must be a rather small hole of howling white savagery. It could not be beautiful or large or bright or able to grow peaches on a tree that someone would water and cultivate, day by day. There could not be people laughing there, or music. What would it mean to buy a new dress, or sip from a cup of coffee, in a place of such unimaginable, deadly intent and accomplishment?

South Africa used to seem so far away. Then it came home to me. It began to signify the meaning of white hatred here. That was what the sheets and the suits and the ties covered up, not very well. That was what the cowardly guys calling me names from their speeding truck wanted to happen to me, to all of me: to my people. That was what would happen to me if I walked around the corner into the wrong neighborhood. That was Birmingham. That was Brooklyn. That was Reagan. That was the end of reason. South Africa was how I came to understand that I am not against war; I am against losing the war.

But war means that you fight. Who is fighting South Africa here, in my house? What am I going to do?

I know my life depends on making this fight my own. As the Harvard psychiatrist Dr. Alvin Poussaint tells me over the phone: "Either you have to strike back or accept your own demise." He is referring, of course, to current joined emergencies that engulf Black life: the ones created by the Reagan administration, which has followed its vicious assault upon domestic social programs with stout declarations of loyalty to the terrorist Botha regime.

"If Reagan can so casually support the death of Black life in Southern Africa, why not here!" says Dr. Poussaint. And I think: "If I accept what Washington and Pretoria impose, then, in a sense, I am already dead."

But I accept none of this. I mean to resist the hatred of these times any way that I can. Squeezed by deadly priorities at home, I am ready to die for the survival of Black people everywhere.

How shall I wage my fight? What can I join? Where are the streets side-to-side jammed with Americans who will not be moved, who will shout until the windows shatter from the walls? Is there a picket line that blocks the South African Embassy? Do the merchants dealing diamonds and gold loudly deny the blood on the counter? Do the students interrupt the teachers who plead ignorance? Do telegrams of outrage blitz the Congress?

No and no and no...What is the difficulty?

Has nobody heard the news? Does no one comprehend that South Africa persists in its defilement of the majority of its people? Does no one see how South Africa expansively exploits its illegal occupation of Namibia? Does no one observe how South Africa pursues its monstrous objectives hundreds of miles into Angola? Does no one realize that Reagan's new African policy supports the murder of hundreds and hundreds of Angolan civilians in the name of "our interests"?

Reeling, beleaguered and terrified by inhumane values carried forward through the actions of this retrograde administration, I yet look for the dignity of an effective, defiant response. I do not believe that we must founder in preoccupations with ourselves as victims, as powerless, and that, therefore, we will no longer rise up and be a mighty people, no matter what the leadership decrees. I do not believe that, in so short a time, Americans have accepted the status of pawns complicit in the crimes of a powerful few and that, accordingly, we can no longer strive to bear witness as a truly righteous people.

South Africa is not so very far away; I am only waiting for the call.

Chapter 3

Many Rivers to Cross
December, 1981

When my mother killed herself I was looking for a job. That was fifteen years ago. I had no money and no food. On the pleasure side I was down to my last pack of Pall Malls plus half a bottle of J & B. I needed to find work because I needed to be able fully to support myself and my eight-year-old son, very fast. My plan was to raise enough big bucks so that I could take an okay apartment inside an acceptable public school district, by September. That deadline left me less than three months to turn my fortunes right side up.

It seemed that I had everything to do at once. Somehow, I must move all of our things, mostly books and toys, out of the housing project before the rent fell due, again. I must do this without letting my neighbors know because destitution and divorce added up to personal shame, and failure. Those same neighbors had looked upon my husband and me as an ideal young couple, in many ways: inseparable, doting, ambitious. They had kept me busy and laughing in the hard weeks following my husband's departure for graduate school in Chicago; they had been the ones to remember him warmly through teasing remarks and questions all that long year that I remained alone, waiting for his return while I became the "temporary," sole breadwinner of our peculiar long-distance family by telephone. They had been the ones who kindly stopped the teasing and the queries when the year ended and my husband, the father of my child, did not come back. They never asked me and I never told them what that meant, altogether. I don't think I really knew.

I could see how my husband would proceed more or less naturally from graduate school to a professional occupation of his

19

choice, just as he had shifted rather easily from me, his wife, to another man's wife—another woman. What I could not see was how I should go forward, now, in any natural, coherent way. As a mother without a husband, as a poet without a publisher, a free-lance journalist without assignment, a city planner without a contract, it seemed to me that several incontestable and conflict-ing necessities had suddenly eliminated the whole realm of choice from my life.

My husband and I agreed that he would have the divorce that he wanted, and I would have the child. This ordinary settlement is, as millions of women will testify, as absurd as saying, "I'll give you a call, you handle everything else." At any rate, as my lawyer explained, the law then was the same as the law today; the courts would surely award me a reasonable amount of the father's income as child support, but the courts would also insist that they could not enforce their own decree. In other words, according to the law, what a father owes to his child is not serious compared to what a man owes to the bank for a car, or a vacation. Hence, as they say, it is extremely regrettable but nonetheless true that the courts cannot garnish a father's salary, nor freeze his account, nor seize his property on behalf of his children, in our society. Appar-ently this is because a child is not a car or a couch or a boat. (I would suppose this is the very best available definition of the difference between an American child and a car.)

Anyway, I wanted to get out of the projects as quickly as possible. But I was going to need help because I couldn't bend down and I couldn't carry anything heavy and I couldn't let my parents know about these problems because I didn't want to fight with them about the reasons behind the problems—which was the same reason I couldn't walk around or sit up straight to read or write without vomiting and acute abdominal pain. My parents would have evaluated that reason as a terrible secret compounded by a terrible crime; once again an unmarried woman, I had, never-theless, become pregnant. What's more I had tried to interrupt this pregnancy even though this particular effort required not only one but a total of three abortions—each of them illegal and amazingly expensive, as well as, evidently, somewhat poorly executed.

My mother, against my father's furious rejections of me and what he viewed as my failure, offered what she could; she had no money herself but there was space in the old brownstone of my childhood. I would live with them during the summer while I pursued my crash schedule for cash, and she would spend as much time with Christopher, her only and beloved grandchild, as her worsening but partially undiagnosed illness allowed.

After she suffered a stroke, her serenely imposing figure had shrunk into an unevenly balanced, starved shell of chronic disorder. In the last two years, her physical condition had forced her retirement from nursing, and she spent most of her days on a makeshift cot pushed against the wall of the dining room next to the kitchen. She could do very few things for herself, besides snack on crackers, or pour ready-made juice into a cup and then drink it.

In June, 1966, I moved from the projects into my parents' house with the help of a woman named Mrs. Hazel Griffin. Since my teens, she had been my hairdresser. Every day, all day, she stood on her feet, washing and straightening hair in her crowded shop, the Arch of Beauty. Mrs. Griffin had never been married, had never finished high school, and she ran the Arch of Beauty with an imperturbable and contagious sense of success. She had a daughter as old as I who worked alongside her mother, coddling customer fantasy into confidence. Gradually, Mrs. Griffin and I became close; as my own mother became more and more bedridden and demoralized, Mrs. Griffin extended herself—dropping by my parents' house to make dinner for them, or calling me to wish me good luck on a special freelance venture, and so forth. It was Mrs. Griffin who closed her shop for a whole day and drove all the way from Brooklyn to my housing project apartment in Queens. It was Mrs. Griffin who packed me up, so to speak, and carried me and the boxes back to Brooklyn, back to the house of my parents. It was Mrs. Griffin who ignored my father standing hateful at the top of the stone steps of the house and not saying a word of thanks and not once relieving her of a single load she wrestled up the stairs and past him. My father hated Mrs. Griffin because he was proud and because she was a stranger of mercy. My father hated Mrs. Griffin because he was like that sometimes: hateful and crazy.

My father alternated between weeping bouts of self-pity and storm explosions of wrath against the gods apparently determined to ruin him. These were his alternating reactions to my mother's increasing enfeeblement, her stoic depression. I think he was scared; who would take care of him? Would she get well again and make everything all right again?

This is how we organized the brownstone; I fixed a room for my son on the top floor of the house. I slept on the parlor floor in the front room. My father slept on the same floor, in the back. My mother stayed downstairs.

About a week after moving in, my mother asked me about the progress of my plans. I told her things were not terrific but that there were two different planning jobs I hoped to secure within a few days. One of them involved a study of new towns in Sweden and the other one involved an analysis of the social consequences of a huge hydro-electric dam under construction in Ghana. My mother stared at me uncomprehendingly and then urged me to look for work in the local post office. We bitterly argued about what she dismissed as my "high-falutin" ideas and, I believe, that was the last substantial conversation between us.

From my first memory of him, my father had always worked at the post office. His favorite was the night shift, which brought him home usually between three and four o'clock in the morning.

It was hot. I finally fell asleep that night, a few nights after the argument between my mother and myself. She seemed to be rallying; that afternoon, she and my son had spent a long time in the backyard, oblivious to the heat and the mosquitoes. They were both tired but peaceful when they noisily re-entered the house, holding hands awkwardly.

But someone was knocking at the door to my room. Why should I wake up? It would be impossible to fall asleep again. It was so hot. The knocking continued. I switched on the light by the bed: 3:30 a.m. It must be my father. Furious, I pulled on a pair of shorts and a t-shirt. "What do you want? What's the matter?" I asked him, through the door. Had he gone berserk? What could he have to talk about at that ridiculous hour?

"OK, all right," I said, rubbing my eyes awake as I stepped to the door and opened it. "What ?"

To my surprise, my father stood there looking very uncertain.

"It's your mother," he told me, in a burly, formal voice. "I think she's dead, but I'm not sure." He was avoiding my eyes.

"What do you mean," I answered.

"I want you to go downstairs and figure it out."

I could not believe what he was saying to me. "You want me to figure out if my mother is dead or alive?"

"I can't tell! I don't know!!" he shouted angrily.

"Jesus Christ," I muttered, angry and beside myself.

I turned and glanced about my room, wondering if I could find anything to carry with me on this mission; what do you use to determine a life or a death? I couldn't see anything obvious that might be useful.

"I'll wait up here," my father said. "You call up and let me know."

I could not believe it; a man married to a woman more than forty years and he can't tell if she's alive or dead and he wakes up his kid and tells her, "You figure it out."

I was at the bottom of the stairs. I halted just outside the dining room where my mother slept. Suppose she really was dead? Suppose my father was not just being crazy and hateful? "Naw," I shook my head and confidently entered the room.

"Momma?!" I called, aloud. At the edge of the cot, my mother was leaning forward, one arm braced to hoist her body up. She was trying to stand up! I rushed over. "Wait. Here, I'll help you!" I said.

And I reached out my hands to give her a lift. The body of my mother was stiff. She was not yet cold, but she was stiff. Maybe I had come downstairs just in time! I tried to loosen her arms, to change her position, to ease her into lying down.

"Momma!" I kept saying. "Momma, listen to me! It's OK! I'm here and everything. Just relax. Relax! Give me a hand, now. I'm trying to help you lie down!"

Her body did not relax. She did not answer me. But she was not cold. Her eyes were not shut.

From upstairs my father was yelling, "Is she dead? Is she dead?"

"No!" I screamed at him. "No! She's not dead!"

At this, my father tore down the stairs and into the room. Then he braked.

"Milly?" he called out, tentative. Then he shouted at me and banged around the walls. "You damn fool. Don't you see now she's gone. Now she's gone!" We began to argue.

"She's alive! Call the doctor!"

"No!"

"Yes!"

At last my father left the room to call the doctor.

I straightened up. I felt completely exhausted from trying to gain a response from my mother. There she was, stiff on the edge of her bed, just about to stand up. Her lips were set, determined. She would manage it, but by herself. I could not help. Her eyes fixed on some point below the floor.

"Momma!" I shook her hard as I could to rouse her into focus. Now she fell back on the cot, but frozen and in the wrong position. It hit me that she might be dead. She might be dead.

My father reappeared at the door. He would not come any closer. "Dr. Davis says he will come. And he call the police."

The police? Would they know if my mother was dead or alive? Who would know?

I went to the phone and called my aunt. "Come quick," I said. "My father thinks Momma has died but she's here but she's stiff."

Soon the house was weird and ugly and crowded and I thought I was losing my mind.

Three white policemen stood around telling me my mother was dead. "How do you know?" I asked, and they shrugged and then they repeated themselves. And the doctor never came. But my aunt came and my uncle and they said she was dead.

After a conference with the cops, my aunt disappeared and when she came back she held a bottle in one of her hands. She and the police whispered together some more. Then one of the cops said, "Don't worry about it. We won't say anything." My aunt signalled me to follow her into the hallway where she let me understand that, in fact, my mother had committed suicide.

I could not assimilate this information: suicide.

I broke away from my aunt and ran to the telephone. I called a friend of mine, a woman who talked back loud to me so that I could realize my growing hysteria, and check it. Then I called my cousin Valerie who lived in Harlem; she woke up instantly and urged me to come right away.

I hurried to the top floor and stood my sleeping son on his feet. I wanted to get him out of this house of death more than I ever wanted anything. He could not stand by himself so I carried him down the two flights to the street and laid him on the backseat and then took off.

At Valerie's, my son continued to sleep, so we put him to bed, closed the door, and talked. My cousin made me eat eggs, drink whiskey, and shower. She would take care of Christopher, she said. I should go back and deal with the situation in Brooklyn.

When I arrived, the house was absolutely full of women from the church dressed as though they were going to Sunday communion. It seemed to me they were, every one of them, wearing hats and gloves and drinking coffee and solemnly addressing invitations to a funeral and I could not find my mother anywhere and I could not find an empty spot in the house where I could sit down and smoke a cigarette.

My mother was dead.

Feeling completely out of place, I headed for the front door, ready to leave. My father grabbed my shoulder from behind and forcibly spun me around.

"You see this?" he smiled, waving a large document in the air. "This am insurance paper for you!" He waved it into my face. "Your mother, she left you insurance, see?"

I watched him.

"But I gwine burn it in the furnace before I give it you to t'row away on trash!"

"Is that money?" I demanded. "Did my mother leave me money?"

"Eh-heh!" he laughed. "And you don't get it from me. Not today, not tomorrow. Not until I dead and buried!"

My father grabbed for my arm and I swung away from him. He hit me on my head and I hit back. We were fighting.

Suddenly, the ladies from the church bustled about and pushed, horrified, between us. This was a sin, they said, for a father and a child to fight in the house of the dead and the mother not yet in the ground! Such a good woman she was, they said. She was a good woman, a good woman, they all agreed. Out of respect for the memory of this good woman, in deference to my mother who had committed suicide, the ladies shook their hats and insisted we should not fight; I should not fight with my father.

Utterly disgusted and disoriented, I went back to Harlem. By the time I reached my cousin's place I had begun to bleed, heavily. Valerie said I was hemorrhaging so she called up her boyfriend and the two of them hobbled me into Harlem Hospital.

I don't know how long I remained unconscious, but when I opened my eyes I found myself on the women's ward, with an intravenous setup feeding into my arm. After a while, Valerie showed up. Christopher was fine, she told me; my friends were taking turns with him. Whatever I did, I should not admit I'd had an abortion or I'd get her into trouble, and myself in trouble. Just play dumb and rest. I'd have to stay on the ward for several days. My mother's funeral was tomorrow afternoon. What did I want her to tell people to explain why I wouldn't be there? She meant, what lie?

I thought about it and I decided I had nothing to say; if I couldn't tell the truth then the hell with it.

I lay in that bed at Harlem Hospital, thinking and sleeping. I wanted to get well.

I wanted to be strong. I never wanted to be weak again as long as I lived. I thought about my mother and her suicide and I thought about how my father could not tell whether she was dead or alive.

I wanted to get well and what I wanted to do as soon as I was strong again, actually, what I wanted to do was I wanted to live my life so that people would know unmistakably that I am alive, so that when I finally die people will know the difference for sure between my living and my death.

And I thought about the idea of my mother as a good woman and I rejected that, because I don't see why it's a good thing when you give up, or when you cooperate with those who hate you or when you polish and iron and mend and endlessly mollify for the sake of the people who love the way that you kill yourself day by day silently.

And I think all of this is really about women and work. Certainly this is all about me as a woman and my life work. I mean I am not sure my mother's suicide was something extraordinary. Perhaps most women must deal with a similar inheritance, the legacy of a woman whose death you cannot possibly pinpoint because she died so many, many times and because, even before she became your mother, the life of that woman was taken; I say it was taken away.

And really it was to honor my mother that I did fight with my father, that man who could not tell the living from the dead.

And really it is to honor Mrs. Hazel Griffin and my cousin Valerie and all the women I love, including myself, that I am working for the courage to admit the truth that Bertolt Brecht has written; he says, "It takes courage to say that the good were defeated not because they were good, but because they were weak."

I cherish the mercy and the grace of women's work. But I know there is new work that we must undertake as well: that new work will make defeat detestable to us. That new women's work will mean we will not die trying to stand up: we will live that way: standing up.

I came too late to help my mother to her feet.

By way of everlasting thanks to all of the women who have helped me to stay alive I am working never to be late again.

Chapter 4

Problems of Language in a Democratic State
1982

In America, you can segregate the people, but the problems will travel. From slavery to equal rights, from state suppression of dissent to crime, drugs and unemployment, I can't think of a single supposedly Black issue that hasn't wasted the original Black target group and then spread like the measles to outlying white experience.

If slavery was all right, for example, if state violence and law could protect property rights against people, then the Bossman could call out the state against striking white workers. And he did. And nobody bothered to track this diseased idea of the state back to the first victims: Black people. Concepts of the state as the equal servant of all the people, as the resource for jobs or subsistence income; concepts of the state as a regulator of the economy to preserve the people from hunger and sickness and doom, these are ideas about a democratic state that have been raised, repeatedly, by minority Americans without majority support.

Most Americans have imagined that problems affecting Black life follow from pathogenic attributes of Black people and not from malfunctions of the state. Most Americans have sought to identify themselves with the powerful interests that oppress poor and minority peoples, perhaps hoping to keep themselves on the shooting side of the target range.

Nevertheless and notwithstanding differences of power, money, race, gender, age and class, there remains one currency common to all of us. There remains one thing that makes possible exchange, shared memory, self-affirmation and collective identity. And isn't that currency known and available to everybody regardless of this and that? And isn't that common currency therefore the basis for a democratic state that will not discriminate between the stronger and the weak? And isn't that indispensable, indiscriminate, or non-discriminating, currency our language? Isn't that so?

I remember very clearly how, when I first became a teacher, back in the 60s, popular wisdom had it that the only American boys and girls who could neither read nor write were Black. This was a function of the poverty of culture or vice versa: I forget which. But anyway, Black children had something wrong with them. They couldn't talk right. They couldn't see straight. They never heard a word you said to them. They seemed to think that they should throw their books around the room or out the windows. And another thing, their parents were no good or they were alcoholics or illiterate or, anyhow, uninterested, inept, and rotten role models.

Obviously, school was cool. It was just the students who kept messing up. In those days teachers were frequently brave, depressed, dedicated, idealistic, tireless, and overworked, but they were never accountable for their failures to teach Black children how to read and write. That was not their responsibility. That was a minority problem of language, in a democratic state.

At the least, most Americans have tried to avoid what they call trouble: opposition to the powerful is a pretty sure way to get yourself in trouble.

But lately these same Americans have begun to understand that trouble does not start somewhere on the other side of town. It seems to originate inside the absolute middle of the homemade cherry pie. In our history, the state has failed to respond to the weak. State power serves the powerful. You could be white, male, Presbyterian and heterosexual besides, but if you get fired or if you get sick tomorrow, you might as well be Black, for all the state will want to hear from you. More and more of the majority is entering that old minority experience of no power: unless you stay strong, state power does not want to sweetly wait upon you.

And when minority problems become the problems of the majority, or when the weak stay weak and the strong become weak, then something does seem to be mighty wrong with the whole situation.

I suggest that as long as state power serves the powerful, more and more of the people of this democracy will become the powerless. As long as we have an economic system protected by the state rather than state protection against economic vagaries and depredations, then your and my welfare become expendable considerations.

Less than two decades after the 60s and I find national reports of a dismal discovery occurring at Harvard, at the nearby community college and on the state campus where I teach. Apparently the minority problem of language has become a majority problem of low-level reading and writing skills. Every university in the nation now recognizes that most of its students seriously lack those analytical abilities that devolve from disciplined and critical and confident and regular exercise of the mind. Students cannot express themselves, clearly. They cannot judge if an essay is gibberish or coherent. They cannot defend a point of view. They cannot examine a written document and then accurately relate its meaning or uncover its purpose. And, either they have nothing to say, or else they talk funny. How did this happen?

I know what went down for Black kids, the ones people dismissed as unruly, unteachable. What those children brought into the classroom: their language, their style, their sense of humor, their ideas of smart, their music, their need for a valid history and a valid literature—history and literature that included their faces and their voices—and serious teachers who would tell them, "C'mon, I see you. Let me give you a hand,"—all of this was pretty well ridiculed and rejected, or denied to them.

Mostly Black kids ran into a censorship of their living particular truth, past and present. Nobody wanted to know what they felt or to teach them to think for themselves. Nobody wanted to learn anything from them. Education was a one-way number leading from the powerful teacher to the trapped parolee. Nobody wanted to hear any more political arguments raised by the fact of certain children whom the compulsory school system consistently failed. Not too many people wanted to grant that maybe schools really are political institutions teaching power to the powerful and something unpalatable and self-destructive to the weak. Not too many people wanted to reexamine their fantasies about the democratizing function of American education.

And when Black dropout rates across the country soared and stabilized at irreversible tragic heights because the kids figured, "If you don't know and don't care about who I am then why should I give a damn about what you say you do know about." The popular wisdom smiled, satisfied: Good riddance to a minority uproar.

But meanwhile, white youngsters fared only somewhat better. These are American kids required to master something described as the English language. These are American kids required to study what's accurately described as English literature. When will a legitimately American language, a language including Nebraska, Harlem, New Mexico, Oregon, Puerto Rico, Alabama and working-class life and freeways and Pac-Man become the language studied and written and glorified in the classroom?

When will a legitimate American literature rightfully supplant nostalgia for Queen Mary? Who teaches white kids to think for themselves? Who has ever wanted white children to see their own faces, clearly, to hear their own voices, clearly?

I believe Americans have wanted their sons and daughters to write just well enough to fill out a job application. Americans have wanted their children to think just well enough to hold that job. Not too many people have wanted to start trouble, or get into it.

So I would say that our schools have served most of us extremely well. We have silenced or eliminated minority children. We have pacified white children into barely competent imitations of their fear-ridden parents.

But now there are no jobs and, consequently, somebody needs to write aggressive new editorials. Somebody needs to write aggressive new statements of social design and demand. More and more Americans finally want to hear new sentences, new ideas, to articulate this unprecedented, and painful, *majority* situation. But is there anybody new around the house? Someone who can think and organize a solution to this loss of privilege, this loss of power?

I am talking about majority problems of language in a democratic state, problems of a currency that someone has stolen and hidden away and then homogenized into an official "English" language that can only express non-events involving nobody responsible, or lies. If we lived in a democratic state our language would have to hurtle, fly, curse, and sing, in all the common American names, all the undeniable and representative and participating voices of everybody here. We would not tolerate the language of the powerful and, thereby, lose all respect for words, *per se*. We would make our language conform to the truth of our many selves and we would make our language lead us into the equality of power that a democratic state must represent.

This is not a democratic state. And we put up with that. We do not have a democratic language. And we put up with that. We have the language of the powerful that perpetuates that power through the censorship of dissenting views.

This morning I watched tv. Four white men sat around talking about some ostensibly important public issue. Everyone of them was wealthy, powerful, unaccountable to you and me and also accustomed to the nationwide delivery of his opinions on a lot of subjects. Except for Tom Wicker, who can't shake his trembling southern drawl for the life of him, they might be quadruplets from an identical Ma and Pa. After about half and hour of this incestuous display, the moderator announced that, after the commercial, he'd send these "experts" out of the studio and replace them with quote a free for all unquote.

I could hardly wait.

After the break, the moderator returned with his new guests: four white men, everyone of them wealthy, powerful, unaccountable to you and me, and also accustomed to the nationwide delivery of his opinions! So much for a quote free for all unquote.

When I say that those particular white men all sounded alike, I am not exaggerating. All of them used the language of the state seeking to transcend accountability to the people, as in: "The Federal Reserve has been forced to raise interest rates" or "It is widely believed..." or "While I can't comment on that I would like to emphasize that it has been said, many times..." or "When you take all of these factors into consideration it is obvious..." or "Unemployment has emerged as a number one concern." Is somebody really saying those words? Is any real life affected by those words? Should we really just relax into the literally non-descript, the irresponsible language of the passive voice? Will the passive voice lead us safely out of the action? Will the action and the actors behind it leave us alone so long as we do not call them by their real names?

We have begun to live in the land of Polyphemus. Poor Polyphemus! He was this ugly and gigantic, one-eyed Cyclops who liked to smash human beings on rocks and then eat them. But one day he happened to capture the wily and very restless Ulysses who, one night, gave Polyphemus so much wine that the poor lunk fell into a drunken sleep. Taking advantage of his adversary's discomposure, Ulysses and a couple of his buddies seized a great stick and heated its tip in the nearby, handily burning, fire. When the tip was glowing hot, Ulysses and his buddies stuck that thing into the one eye of Polyphemus, twisting it deeply into that socket, and blinding him.

Polyphemus howled a terrible loud howl. He was in much pain. "What is the name of the man who has done this to me?" he cried. And the wily Ulysses answered him, "My name is No One."

Later, several other Cyclops raced up to Polyphemus, because they had heard him howling.

"Who did this to you?" they asked.

Polyphemus screamed his accusation for the world to hear: "No One has done this to me!"

Well, when the fellow Cyclops heard that they decided that if No One had done this to Polyphemus, it must be the will of the gods. Hence nothing could or should be done about the blinding of Polyphemus. And so nothing was done.

And after a while, Ulysses and his men escaped, unnoticed by the blinded Cyclops.

I share this story with you because it remains one of my favorites and because it was the only reason I stayed awake during my second year of Latin.

And I tell you about Polyphemus because we seem determined to warp ourselves into iddy-biddy imitations of his foolishness. To repeat: the other Cyclops decided that if no one had done anything then nothing was to be done. What happened to him represented the will of the gods.

I worry about that notion of a democratic state. Do we really believe 11.5% unemployment represents God's will? Is that why the powerful say, "Unemployment has emerged?" If that construction strikes your ear as somehow ridiculous because, quite rightly, it conjures up the phenomenon of unemployment as if it emerges from nowhere into nothing, then what sense do you make of this very familiar construction used, very often, by the power-*less:* "I lost my job." Who in his or her right mind loses a job? What should I understand if you say something like that to me? Should I suppose that one morning you got up and drank your coffee and left the house but, then, you just couldn't find your job? If that's not what anybody means then why don't we say, "GM laid off half the night shift. They fired me."

Who did what to whom? Who's responsible?

We have a rather foggy mess and not much hope for a democratic state when the powerless agree to use a language that blames the victim for the deeds of the powerful.

As in: "I was raped." What should we conclude from that most sadly passive use of language? By definition, nobody in her right mind can say that, and mean it. For rape to occur, somebody real has to rape somebody else, equally real. Rape presupposes a rapist and his victim. The victim must learn to make language tell her own truth: He raped me.

But the victim accomodates to power. The victim doesn't want anymore trouble; someone has already fired him or someone has already raped her, and so the victim uses words to evade a further confrontation with the powerful.

By itself, our language cannot refuse to reflect the agonizing process of alienation from ourselves. If we collaborate with the powerful then our language will lose its currency as a means to tell the truth in order to change the truth.

In our own passive ways, we frequently validate the passive voice of a powerful state that seeks to conceal the truth from us, the people. And this seems to me an ok situation only for a carnivorous idiot like Polyphemus.

I would not care if, for example, instead of bashing men's heads against the rocks, Polyphemus decided to watch tv, every evening. I wouldn't even care if he, consequently, became addicted to that ultimate passive experience, although maybe that's why he thought that when you murder somebody it's not such a big deal: the agony will last only a couple of minutes until the much more exciting drama of Ajax the Foaming Cleanser takes over the screen. Some people *should* be pacified. Polyphemus was one of those.

But I really think that a democratic state presupposes a small number of psychopathic giants and a rather huge number of ordinary men and women who cannot afford to resemble Polyphemus.

In September of this year, a huge number of ordinary men and women came out of their houses to make an outcry against the language of the state. Four hundred thousand Israelis plunged into the streets of Tel Aviv to demand an investigation of the massacre in Lebanon. They insisted. They must know: who did what to whom?

Against official pronouncements such as: "Security measures have been taken," or "It seems that an incident has taken place inside the camps," nearly half a million Israelis, after the massacre at Sabra and Shatilah, demanded another kind of language: an inquiry into the truth, an attribution of responsibility, a forcing of the powerful into an accountability to the people. As Jacobo Timmerman writes in his Israeli *Journal of the Longest War*, it did seem to him that the democratic nature of the state lay at risk.

All the summer leading to Sabra and Shatilah I lived with the Israeli invasion of Lebanon. It did not kill me. As Timmerman has described our remarkable endurance of the unendurable, "...nobody has yet died of anguish." But that invasion killed other people: tens of thousands died and I watched it happen. I sat down and I read the newspaper accounts or I listened to the nightly news. The uniformity of official state language appalled me. How could this be 1984 in 1982?

I saw American reporters respectfully quote Philip Habib as having proclaimed, "This is a ceasefire" even as the whistling bombs drowned out the broadcast. When Menachem Begin declared,
"This is not an invasion," his statement appeared in print and on the screen, everywhere as the world news of the day, even as the Israeli tanks entered Beirut.

During that same September, 1982, and shortly before Sabra and Shatilah, Israeli planes bombed the houses and the hospitals and the schools of West Beirut for twenty-two hours, unceasingly. But this was something, evidently, other than a massacre. Our American newspapers and newsmen told us that this was a "tightening of the noose" in order to "speed negotiations at the peace table."

But when one word finally burst through that foggy mess of American mass media, and when that word was *massacre*, who took it to the streets? Who called for an investigation of the government and moved to put the leadership on trial? Who said *stop*?

It happened in another country where the citizens believe it matters when the state controls the language. It didn't happen here. It happened when the citizens decided that the passive voice in a democracy means something evil way beyond a horribly mixed metaphor. It didn't happen here.

It happened in Israel. And we Americans should be ashamed.

But we were looking for a language of the people; we were wondering why our children do not read or write.

Last week a delegation of Black women graduate students invited me to address a large meeting that loud yellow flyers

described as "A Black Sisters Speak-Out" followed by two excla-
mation point. I went to the gathering with great excitement.
Obviously, we would deal with one or another crisis; whether
national or international, I simply wondered which enormous and
current quandary would be the one most of the women wanted to to
discuss.

During the warm-up period one of the women announced that
we should realize our debt to the great Black women who have
preceeded us in history. "We are here," she said, "because of the
struggle of women like," and here her sentence broke down. She
tried again. "We have come this far because of all the Black women
who fought for us like, like..." and, here, only one name came to her
mouth: "Sojourner Truth!" she exclaimed, clearly relieved to think
of it, but, also embarassed because she couldn't keep going
"And," she tried to continue, nevertheless, "the other Black
women like...but here somebody in the audience spoke to her
rescue, by calling aloud the name of Harriet Tubman. At this point
I interrupted to observe that now we had *two* names for *482* years
of our Afro-American history.

"What about Mary McLeod Bethune?" somebody else ven-
tured at last. "That's three!" I remarked, in the manner of a referee:
"Do we have a fourth?"

There was silence. Thoroughly embarassed, the first woman
looked at me and said, "Listen. I could come up with a whole list of
Black women if my life depended on it."

"Well," I had to tell her, "It does."

But even this official erasure of their faces and their voices
was not what those students wanted to discuss. Something more
hurtful than that was bothering them. As one by one these Black
women rose to express themselves, the problem was this:

A lotta times and I'm walking on campus and I see
another Black woman and so I'll say 'Hi' but then she
won't answer me and I don't understand it because I don't
mean we have to get into a conversation or do all of that
like talking to me but you could say, 'Hi.' If you see me you
could say, 'Hi.'

I was stunned. From looking around the room I knew there were
Black women right there who face critical exposure to bodily
assault, alcoholic mothers, and racist insults and graffiti in the
dorms. I knew that the academic curriculum omitted the truth of
their difficult lives. I knew that they certainly would not be found
welcome in the marketplace after they got their degrees.

But the insistent concern was more intimate and more pitiful and more desperate than any of those threatening conditions might sugest. The abject plea of those Black women students was ruthlessly minimal: "If you see me, you could say, '*Hi.*' Let me know that you see me; let me know I exist. Never mind a conversation between us, but, please, if you see me, you could say, *"Hi."*

Who can tell these Americans that they should trust the language available to them? Who will presume to criticize their faltering, their monosyllables, their alienation from a literature that condemns them to oblivion?

If you choose, you can consider this desperation a minority problem in America, today, and then try to forget about it. But I believe this invisibility and this silence of the real and various peoples of our country is a political situation of language that every one of us must move against, because our lives depend on it.

I believe we will have to eliminate the passive voice from our democracy. We will have to drown out the official language of the powerful with our own mighty and conflicting voices or we will perish as a people. Until we can tell our children that the powerful people are the children, themselves, then I do not see why we should expect our children to read or write anything.

Until we can tell our children that truth is the purpose of our American language, and that the truth is what they know and feel and need, then I believe our children will continue to act as though the truth is just something that will get you into trouble.

I believe that somebody real has blinded America in at least one eye. And, in the same way that so many Americans feel that "we have lost our jobs," we suspect that we have lost our country.

We know that we do not speak the language.

And I ask you: well, what are we going to do about it?

Chapter 5

The Case for the Real Majority
1982

In the United States, race and class are fixed correlatives, despite occasional noise to the contrary. For Black people, this correlation has meant the last and the least of available national resources, throughout our hated presence here. Right now, our national income represents a severely declining percentage of what our white counterparts enjoy.

This is known.

What begs for programmatic and rapid recognition is the equally important correlation between gender and class. Most of the American poor, white and Black, are women.

What is not anywhere acknowledged, to date, is the specific composition of us, as a people. Most Black Americans are Black women. Most Black women occupy the lowest paid, lowest status jobs in our society, when they can get a job. When they can't, they occupy the ranks of the most unemployed. (Bear in mind that, to be counted among the unemployed, you must actively seek work and not, as the media construct the fairytale, whimsically evade really swell opportunities to make a living wage.) Most Black children are raised by these same Black women who receive the least imaginable social and economic support even while they must endure the savage consequences of the most absurd theoretical censure by endlessly various male experts who, I have noticed, never offer to throw themselves in front of fast moving trains or trucks in order to stop the insanity of a killer system built upon the unpaid as well as the deliberately lowest paid labor of more than half of its citizens: the women.

If any of us hopes to survive, s/he must meet the extremity of the American female condition with immediate and political response. The thoroughly destructive and indefensible subjugation of the majority of Americans cannot continue except at the peril of the entire body politic. You might suppose this would be obvious to everyone talking about Freedom and Rights and Equality and Justice and The Spirit and The Future. But, apparently, this enormous and simple idea, the idea that the welfare of the majority will determine the welfare of the state, becomes an impossible concept to assimilate—once the majority has been identified as female.

In like manner, the penalties attached to Black womanhood threaten all Black people with ignominious extinction. Think about that. Think about "Black people" without most of us caring for and about the rest of you. Think about "Black people" without most of our children growing up able to eat and able to read what they need to take on the world, eye to eye.

Overall, white men run America. From nuclear armaments to the filth and jeopardy of New York City subways to the cruel mismanagement of health care, is there anything to boast about? Any safety and grace of a growing nature to claim? Is there any major and worldwide and man-made hazard to human life that cannot be traced to the willful activities of white men?

Overall, Black men dominate Black America. The leading cause of death for Black men ages twenty-five to forty-four is murder by other Black men! What is the leading cause of sorrow for Black women? What is the leading cause of grief in the hearts of our children?

The huge and dire truth about white and Black American women is trivial compared to what will happen to each of us if we refuse to transform this evil situation into a past reminder of a close call with collective death.

As Americans we live in danger for our lives. As Black people we live in the valley of the shadow of deth. I say look to the welfare of the majority—the women—if you would save yourself.

Chapter 6

Report from the Bahamas
1982

I am staying in a hotel that calls itself The Sheraton British
Colonial. One of the photographs advertising the place displays a
middle-aged Black man in a waiter's tuxedo, smiling. What
intrigues me most about the picture is just this: while the Black
man bears a tray full of "colorful" drinks above his left shoulder,
both of his feet, shoes and trouserlegs, up to ten inches above his
ankles, stand in the also "colorful" Caribbean salt water. He is so
delighted to serve you he will wade into the water to bring you
Banana Daquiris while you float! More precisely, he will wade into
the water, fully clothed, oblivious to the ruin of his shoes, his
trousers, his health, and he will do it with a smile.

I am in the Bahamas. On the phone in my room, a spinning
complement of plastic pages offers handy index clues such as CAR
RENTAL and CASINOS. A message from the Ministry of Tour-
ism appears among these travellers tips. Opening with a paragraph of "WELCOME," the message then proceeds to "A PAGE
OF HISTORY," which reads as follows:

> New World History begins on the same day that modern
> Bahamian history begins—October 12, 1492. That's
> when Columbus stepped ashore—British influence came
> first with the Eleutherian Adventurers of 1647—After the
> Revolutions, American Loyalists fled from the newly
> independent states and settled in the Bahamas. Confed-
> erate blockade-runners used the island as a haven

during the War between the States, and after the War, a
number of Southerners moved to the Bahamas...

There it is again. Something proclaims itself a legitimate history
and all it does is track white Mr. Columbus to the British
Eleutherians through the Confederate Southerners as they barge
into New World surf, land on New World turf, and nobody saying
one word about the Bahamian people, the Black peoples, to whom
the only thing new in their island world was this weird succession
of crude intruders and its colonial consequences.

This is my consciousness of race as I unpack my bathing suit
in the Sheraton British Colonial. Neither this hotel nor the British
nor the long ago Italians nor the white Delta airline pilots belong
here, of course. And every time I look at the photograph of that fool
standing in the water with his shoes on I'm about to have a West
Indian fit, even though I know he's no fool; he's a middle-aged
Black man who needs a job and this is his job—pretending himself
a servile ancillary to the pleasures of the rich. (Compared to his
options in life, I am a rich woman. Compared to most of the Black
Americans arriving for this Easter weekend on a three nights four
days' deal of bargain rates, the middleaged waiter is a poor Black
man.)

We will jostle along with the other (white) visitors and join
them in the tee shirt shops or, laughing together, learn ruthless
rules of negotiation as we, Black Americans as well as white,
argue down the price of handwoven goods at the nearby straw
market while the merchants, frequently toothless Black women
seated on the concrete in their only presentable dress, humble
themselves to our careless games:

"Yes? You like it? Eight dollar."

"Five."

"I give it to you. Seven."

And so it continues, this weird succession of crude intruders
that, now, includes me and my brothers and my sisters from the
North.

This is my consciousness of class as I try to decide how much
money I can spend on Bahamian gifts for my family back in
Brooklyn. No matter that these other Black women incessantly
weave words and flowers into the straw hats and bags piled beside
them on the burning dusty street. No matter that these other Black
women must work their sense of beauty into these things that we
will take away as cheaply as we dare, or they will do without food.

We are not white, after all. The budget is limited. And we are harmlessly killing time between the poolside rum punch and "The Native Show on the Patio" that will play tonight outside the hotel restaurant.

This is my consciousness of race and class and gender identity as I notice the fixed relations between these other Black women and myself. They sell and I buy or I don't. They risk not eating. I risk going broke on my first vacation afternoon.

We are not particularly women anymore; we are parties to a transaction designed to set us against each other.

"Olive" is the name of the Black woman who cleans my hotel room. On my way to the beach I am wondering what "Olive" would say if I told her why I chose The Sheraton British Colonial; if I told her I wanted to swim. I wanted to sleep. I did not want to be harassed by the middleaged waiter, or his nephew. I did not want to be raped by anybody (white or Black) at all and I calculated that my safety as a Black woman alone would best be assured by a multinational hotel corporation. In my experience, the big guys take customer complaints more seriously than the little ones. I would suppose that's one reason why they're big; they don't like to lose money anymore than I like to be bothered when I'm trying to read a goddamned book underneath a palm tree I paid $264 to get next to. A Black woman seeking refuge in a multinational corporation may seem like a contradiction to some, but there you are. In this case it's a coincidence of entirely different self-interests: Sheraton/cash = June Jordan's short run safety.

Anyway, I'm pretty sure "Olive" would look at me as though I came from someplace as far away as Brooklyn. Then she'd probably allow herself one indignant query before righteously removing her vacuum cleaner from my room; "and why in the first place you come down you without your husband?"

I cannot imagine how I would begin to answer her.

My "rights" and my "freedom" and my "desire" and a slew of other New World values; what would they sound like to this Black woman described on the card atop my hotel bureau as "Olive the Maid"? "Olive" is older than I am and I may smoke a cigarette while she changes the sheets on my bed. Whose rights? Whose freedom? Whose desire?

And why should she give a shit about mine unless I do something, for real, about hers?

It happens that the book that I finished reading under a palm tree earlier today was the novel, *The Bread Givers*, by Anzia Yezierska. Definitely autobiographical, Yezierska lays out the difficulties of being both female and "a person" inside a traditional Jewish family at the start of the 20th century. That any Jewish woman became anything more than the abused servant of her father or her husband is really an improbable piece of news. Yet Yezierska managed such an unlikely outcome for her own life. In *The Bread Givers*, the heroine also manages an important, although partial, escape from traditional Jewish female destiny. And in the unpardonable, despotic father, the Talmudic scholar of that Jewish family, did I not see my own and hate him twice, again? When the heroine, the young Jewish child, wanders the streets with a filthy pail she borrows to sell herring in order to raise the ghetto rent and when she cries, "Nothing was before me but the hunger in our house, and no bread for the next meal if I didn't sell the herring. No longer like a fire engine, but like a houseful of hungry mouths my heart cried, 'herring—herring! Two cents apiece!'" who would doubt the ease, the sisterhood of conversation possible between that white girl and the Black women selling straw bags on the streets of paradise because they do not want to die? And is it not obvious that the wife of that Talmudic scholar and "Olive," who cleans my room here at the hotel, have more in common than I can claim with either one of them?

This is my consciousness of race and class and gender identity as I collect wet towels, sunglasses, wristwatch, and head towards a shower.

I am thinking about the boy who loaned this novel to me. He's white and he's Jewish and he's pursuing an independent study project with me, at the State University where I teach whether or not I feel like it, where I teach without stint because, like the waiter, I am no fool. It's my job and either I work or I do without everything you need money to buy. The boy loaned me the novel because he thought I'd be interested to know how a Jewish-American writer used English so that the syntax, and therefore the cultural habits of mind expressed by the Yiddish language, could survive translation. He did this because he wanted to create another connection between us on the basis of language, between his knowledge/his love of Yiddish and my knowledge/my love of Black English.

He has been right about the forceful survival of the Yiddish. And I had become excited by this further evidence of the written voice of spoken language protected from the monodrone of "standard" English, and so we had grown closer on this account. But then our talk shifted to student affairs more generally, and I had learned that this student does not care one way or the other about currently jeopardized Federal Student Loan Programs because, as he explained it to me, they do not affect him. He does not need financial help outside his family. My own son, however, is Black. And I am the only family help available to him and that means, if Reagan succeeds in eliminating Federal programs to aid minority students, he will have to forget about furthering his studies, or he or I or both of us will have to hit the numbers pretty big. For these reasons of difference, the student and I had moved away from each other, even while we continued to talk.

My consciousness turned to race, again, and class.

Sitting in the same chair as the boy, several weeks ago, a graduate student came to discuss her grade. I praised the excellence of her final paper; indeed it had seemed to me an extraordinary pulling together of recent left brain/right brain research with the themes of transcendental poetry.

She told me that, for her part, she'd completed her reading of my political essays. "You are so lucky!" she exclaimed.

"What do you mean by that?"

"You have a cause. You have a purpose to your life."

I looked carefully at this white woman; what was she really saying to me?

"What do you mean?" I repeated.

"Poverty. Police violence. Discrimination in general."

(Jesus Christ, I thought: Is that her idea of lucky?)

"And how about you?" I asked.

"Me?"

"Yeah, you. Don't you have a cause?"

"Me? I'm just a middle aged woman: a housewife and a mother. I'm a nobody."

For a while, I made no response.

First of all, speaking of race and class and gender in one breath, what she said meant that those lucky preoccupations of mine, from police violence to nuclear wipe-out, were not shared. They were mine and not hers. But here she sat, friendly as an old stuffed animal, beaming good will or more "luck" in my direction.

In the second place, what this white woman said to me meant that she did not believe she was "a person" precisely because she had fulfilled the traditional female functions revered by the father of that Jewish immigrant, Anzia Yezierska. And the woman in front of me was not a Jew. That was not the connection. The link was strictly female. Nevertheless, how should that woman and I, another female connect, beyond this bizarre exchange?

If she believed me lucky to have regular hurdles of discrimination then why shouldn't I insist that she's lucky to be a middle class white Wasp female who lives in such well-sanctioned and normative comfort that she even has the luxury to deny the power of the privileges that paralyze her life?

If she deserts me and "my cause" where we differ, if, for example, she abandons me to "my" problems of race, then why should I support her in "her" problems of housewifely oblivion?

Recollection of this peculiar moment brings me to the shower in the bathroom cleaned by "Olive." She reminds me of the usual Women's Studies curriculum because it has nothing to do with her or her job: you won't find "Olive" listed anywhere on the reading list. You will likewise seldom hear of Anzia Yezierska. But yes, you will find, from Florence Nightingale to Adrienne Rich, a white procession of independently well-to-do women writers. (Gertrude Stein/Virginia Woolf/Hilda Doolittle are standard names among the "essential" women writers).

In other words, most of the women of the world—Black and First World and white who work because we must—most of the women of the world persist far from the heart of the usual Women's Studies syllabus.

Similarly, the typical Black History course will slide by the majority experience it pretends to represent. For example, Mary McLeod Bethune will scarcely receive as much attention as Nat Turner, even though Black women who bravely and efficiently provided for the education of Black people hugely outnumber those few Black men who led successful or doomed rebellions against slavery. In fact, Mary McLeod Bethune may not receive even honorable mention because Black History too often apes those ridiculous white history courses which produce such dangerous gibberish as The Sheraton British Colonial "history" of the Bahamas. Both Black and white history courses exclude from their central consideration those people who neither killed nor conquered anyone as the means to new identity, those people who took care of every one of the people who wanted to become "a person," those people who still take care of the life at issue: the ones who wash and who feed and who teach and who diligently

decorate straw hats and bags with all of their historically
unrequired gentle love: the women.

Oh the old rugged cross
on a hill far away
Well I cherish the old rugged cross

It's Good Friday in the Bahamas. Seventy-eight degrees in the
shade. Except for Sheraton territory, everything's closed.

It so happens that for truly secular reasons I've been fasting
for three days. My hunger has now reached nearly violent
proportions. In the hotel sandwich shop, the Black woman
handling the counter complains about the tourists; why isn't the
shop closed and why don't the tourists stop eating for once in their
lives. I'm famished and I order chicken salad and cottage cheese
and lettuce and tomato and a hard boiled egg and a hot cross bun
and apple juice.

She eyes me with disgust.

To be sure, the timing of my stomach offends her serious
religious practices. Neither one of us apologizes to the other. She
seasons the chicken salad to the peppery max while I listen to the
loud radio gospel she plays to console herself. It's a country Black
version of "The Old Rugged Cross."

As I heave much chicken into my mouth tears start. It's not
the pepper. I am, after all, a West Indian daughter. It's the Good
Friday music that dominates the humid atmosphere.

Well I cherish the old rugged cross

And I am back, faster than a 747, in Brooklyn, in the home of my
parents where we are wondering, as we do every year, if the sky
will darken until Christ has been buried in the tomb. The sky
should darken if God is in His heavens. And then, around 3 p.m., at
the conclusion of our mournful church service at the neighborhood
St. Phillips, and even while we dumbly stare at the black cloth
covering the gold altar and the slender unlit candles, the sun
should return through the high gothic windows and vindicate our
waiting faith that the Lord will rise again, on Easter.

How I used to bow my head at the very name of Jesus: ecstatic
to abase myself in deference to His majesty.

My mouth is full of salad. I can't seem to eat quickly enough. I
can't think how I should lessen the offense of my appetite. The
other Black woman on the premises, the one who disapprovingly
prepared this very tasty break from my fast, makes no remark. She
is no fool. This is a job that she needs. I suppose she notices that at

least I included a hot cross bun among my edibles. That's something in my favor. I decide that's enough.

I am suddenly eager to walk off the food. Up a fairly steep hill I walk without hurrying. Through the pastel desolation of the little town, the road brings me to a confectionary pink and white plantation house. At the gates, an unnecessarily large statue of Christopher Columbus faces me down, or tries to. His hand is fisted to one hip. I look back at him, laugh without deference, and turn left.

It's time to pack it up. Catch my plane. I scan the hotel room for things not to forget. There's that white report card on the bureau.

"Dear Guests:" it says, under the name "Olive." I am your maid for the day. Please rate me: Excellent. Good. Average. Poor. Thank you."

I tuck this momento from the Sheraton British Colonial into my notebook. How would "Olive" rate *me*? What would it mean for us to seem "good" to each other? What would that rating require?

But I am hastening to leave. Neither turtle soup nor kidney pie nor any conch shell delight shall delay my departure. I have rested, here, in the Bahamas, and I'm ready to return to my usual job, my usual work. But the skin on my body has changed and so has my mind. On the Delta flight home I realize I am burning up, indeed.

So far as I can see, the usual race and class concepts of connection, or gender assumptions of unity, do not apply very well. I doubt that they ever did. Otherwise why would Black folks forever bemoan our lack of solidarity when the deal turns real. And if unity on the basis of sexual oppression is something natural, then why do we women, the majority people on the planet, still have a problem?

The plane's ready for takeoff. I fasten my seatbelt and let the tumult inside my head run free. Yes: race and class and gender remain as real as the weather. But what they must mean about the contact between two individuals is less obvious and, like the weather, not predictable.

And when these factors of race and class and gender absolutely collapse is whenever you try to use them as automatic concepts of connection. They may serve well as indicators of commonly felt conflict, but as elements of connection they seem about as reliable as precipitation probability for the day after the night before the day.

It occurs to me that much organizational grief could be avoided if people understood that partnership in misery does not necessarily provide for partnership for change: *When we get the monsters off our backs all of us may want to run in very different directions.*

And not only that: even though both "Olive" and "I" live inside a conflict neither one of us created, and even though both of us therefore hurt inside that conflict, I may be one of the monsters she needs to eliminate from her universe and, in a sense, she may be one of the monsters in mine.

I am reaching for the words to describe the difference between a common identity that has been imposed and the individual identity any one of us will choose, once she gains that chance.

That difference is the one that keeps us stupid in the face of new, specific information about somebody else with whom we are supposed to have a connection because a third party, hostile to both of us, has worked it so that the two of us, like it or not, share a common enemy. *What happens beyond the idea of that enemy and beyond the consequences of that enemy?*

I am saying that the ultimate connection cannot be the enemy. The ultimate connection must be the need that we find between us. It is not only who you are, in other words, but what we can do for each other that will determine the connection.

I am flying back to my job. I have been teaching contemporary women's poetry this semester. One quandary I have set myself to explore with my students is the one of taking responsibility without power. We had been wrestling ideas to the floor for several sessions when a young Black woman, a South African, asked me for help, after class.

Sokutu told me she was "in a trance" and that she'd been unable to eat for two weeks.

"What's going on?" I asked her, even as my eyes startled at her trembling and emaciated appearance.

"My husband. He drinks all the time. He beats me up. I go to the hospital. I can't eat. I don't know what/anything."

In my office, she described her situation. I did not dare to let her sense my fear and horror. She was dragging about, hour by hour, in dread. Her husband, a young Black South African, was drinking himself into more and more deadly violence against her.

Sokutu told me how she could keep nothing down. She weighed 90 lbs. at the outside, as she spoke to me. She'd already been hospitalized as a result of her husband's battering rage.

I knew both of them because I had organized a campus group to aid the liberation struggles of Southern Africa.

Nausea rose in my throat. What about this presumable connection: this husband and this wife fled from that homeland of hatred against them, and now what? He was destroying himself. If not stopped, he would certainly murder his wife.

She needed a doctor, right away. It was a medical emergency. She needed protection. It was a security crisis. She needed refuge for battered wives and personal therapy and legal counsel. She needed a friend.

I got on the phone and called every number in the campus directory that I could imagine might prove helpful. Nothing worked. There were no institutional resources designed to meet her enormous, multifaceted, and ordinary woman's need.

I called various students. I asked the Chairperson of the English Department for advice. I asked everyone for help.

Finally, another one of my students, Cathy, a young Irish woman active in campus IRA activities, responded. She asked for further details. I gave them to her.

"Her husband," Cathy told me, "is an alcoholic. You have to understand about alcoholics. It's not the same as anything else. And it's a disease you can't treat any old way.

I listened, fearfully. Did this mean there was nothing we could do?

"That's not what I'm saying," she said. "But you have to keep the alcoholic part of the thing central in everybody's mind, otherwise her husband will kill her. Or he'll kill himself."

She spoke calmly, I felt there was nothing to do but to assume she knew what she was talking about.

"Will you come with me?" I asked her, after a silence. "Will you come with me and help us figure out what to do next?"

Cathy said she would but that she felt shy: Sokutu comes from South Africa. What would she think about Cathy?

"I don't know," I said. "But let's go."

We left to find a dormitory room for the young battered wife.

It was late, now, and dark outside.

On Cathy's VW that I followed behind with my own car, was the sticker that reads BOBBY SANDS FREE AT LAST. My eyes blurred as I read and reread the words. This was another connection: Bobby Sands and Martin Luther King Jr. and who would believe it? I would not have believed it; I grew up terrorized by Irish kids who introduced me to the word "nigga."

And here I was following an Irish woman to the room of a Black South African. We were going to that room to try to save a life together.

When we reached the little room, we found ourselves awkward and large. Sokutu attempted to treat us with utmost courtesy, as though we were honored guests. She seemed surprised by Cathy, but mostly Sokutu was flushed with relief and joy because we were there, with her.

I did not know how we should ever terminate her heartfelt courtesies and address, directly, the reason for our visit: her starvation and her extreme physical danger.

Finally, Cathy sat on the floor and reached out her hands to Sokutu.

"I'm here," she said quietly, "Because June has told me what has happened to you. And I know what it is. Your husband is an alcoholic. He has a disease. I know what it is. My father was an alcoholic. He killed himself. He almost killed my mother. I want to be your friend."

"Oh," was the only small sound that escaped from Sokutu's mouth. And then she embraced the other student. And then everything changed and I watched all of this happen so I know that this happened: this connection.

And after we called the police and exchanged phone numbers and plans were made for the night and for the next morning, the young South African woman walked down the dormitory hallway, saying goodbye and saying thank you to us.

I walked behind them, the young Irish woman and the young South African, and I saw them walking as sisters walk, hugging each other, and whispering and sure of each other and I felt how it was not who they were but what they both know and what they were both preparing to do about what they know that was going to make them both free at last.

And I look out the windows of the plane and I see clouds that will not kill me and I know that someday soon other clouds may erupt to kill us all.

And I tell the stewardess No thanks to the cocktails she offers me. But I look about the cabin at the hundred strangers drinking as they fly and I think even here and even now I must make the connection real between me and these strangers everywhere before those other clouds unify this ragged bunch of us, too late.

Chapter 7

Love is Not the Problem
February, 1983

In between classes and in the middle of campus, I met him on a
very cold day. He stood, without shivering, behind a small table on
which an anti-McCarthy petition and pages of signatures lay,
blowing about. He wore no overcoat, no gloves, no scarf, and I
noticed that his cheeks seemed almost bitterly red with the wind.
Although that happened some twenty-eight years ago, I remember
that he wore a bright yellow Oxford cloth button-down shirt, open
at the neck, and no tie. He explained the petition to me. But I
wanted to do something else. I wanted to excuse myself and find
him a cup of coffee so he'd keep warm enough to continue standing
out there, brave against Senator Joe McCarthy and the the witch-
hunts that terrorized America. He looked like a hero to me. It really
was cold. He really didn't care. He stood there, by himself, on
purpose. I went away to bring him back a cup of coffee, and, as I
recall, that same afternoon I told a couple of my friends that I had
met the man I would marry.

That was 1954. He was a twenty-year-old senior at Columbia
College. I was eighteen and a sophomore at Barnard College,
across the street. It would be hard to say which one of us was
younger or more ignorant of the world beyond our books, our
NAACP meetings, school parties, ping-pong, running hikes
through Van Cortlandt Park, or our exhaustively romantic letter-
writing at the rate of two or three letters a day. But he was taller
and stronger, and he was white. We were not the same.

In 1954, the United States Supreme Court ruled, in *Brown vs.
Board of Education,* that "separate" was not "equal," that segre-
gated schools delivered an inferior education to the children of the

dominated. The court found that Black children needed to inte-
grate with the children of the dominating American groups—
white children—in order to secure a decently acceptable education.

Although this decision did not arrive with trumpets sounding,
it surely prefigured the revolutionary nature of the next twenty
years of American history. "Separate but unequal" became the
gathering outcry of millions of Black people as everything imposed upon us, all forms of hatred and discrimination, became
coherently recognizable inside that single concept. Integration
with the powerful became the tactic and the strategy for equal
rights.

I happen to believe that analysis was off. Rather than struggling to share in a patently evil kind of power, the power of people
who will demean and destroy those who are weaker than they, I
think we might, more usefully, have sought to redefine that meaning of power, altogether.

But I was not thinking about law or theory of any kind when,
in 1955, I married my young man from across the street. My
parents utterly opposed the marriage. His parents opposed the
marriage. Our friends (an unruly mix of Black and white students)
thought we must be kidding: why get married? Nobody thought
either of us was old enough to do anything so serious as that. (And
I would have to agree with them, at this remove.) But our friends
came. The Episcopal minister came. At the last minute, my parents came. His parents did not. And we got married to the accom-
paniment of wedding presents that included the four-volume
Social History of Art and a snakebite kit for camping.

Now I look back on those two kids who fell in love and went
ahead and married each other, he wearing an awkwardly fitted
but spotless tuxedo and she wearing the highest spike heels and
the best $35 wedding gown from Brooklyn, and both of them, in
every sense, obvious virgins in a cruel land. From that moment in
1955, where, I wonder, should the cameras cut? To the white mothers screaming invectives at fifteen year old Elizabeth Eckford as
she approached the school yard in Little Rock, Arkansas? To the
mutilated bodies of the Black and white SNCC volunteers found
below the Mississippi highway? To the Birmingham police and
the police dogs and that white violence that killed the four Black
children in the Birmingham church?

Thinking only about what to wear, exactly, or what reading to
pack on the honeymoon trip they couldn't afford and about brand
new sleeping bags, those two kids quietly did something against

the law, against every tradition, against the power arrangements of this country: they loved each other.

Apparently, this is where the rest of us get into the story. When two people do something the rest of us don't like or some of us feel real nosy about, then the rest of us interpose ourselves in any way we can. We call out the law. We produce experts. We maintain an attitude. We ostracize. We whisper. We develop jargon such as Interracial Marriage or Sleeping White or Niggah Lover or Identity Conflict or Acting Out or Patterns of Rebellion. And if possible, we kill them, the ones who love each other despite sacrosanct rules of enmity and hatred.

Well, my marriage to that young man from across the street lasted ten and a half years, which is, of course, longer than many. And I think ours was more interesting in some ways. And I know that in America, one out of two marriages fails nowadays: the institution itself is not well, evidently. And I know that I do not regret my marriage. Nor do I regret my divorce.

Hardly anyone talks about love anymore, but I know that I did love that particular young man and that he loved me. And I know that despite the varieties of racist resistance to such love, the number of men and women entering Black and white interracial marriage more than doubled from 1970 to 1980. And, on the campus where I teach, I see an increasing number of young people who are interacting with each other, as Black and white friends and lovers.

But as a university teacher for the past sixteen years, I have also learned how extremely few of anyone's children are either happy or clear or confident. Most of our children suffer from an agonizing lack of self-respect and a critical absence of faith in anyone or anything.

I think that the children of love between somebody Black and somebody white will probably know burdens beyond the enormous "normal" difficulties of growing up in a rather insane, internecine society. As my own son puts it, "There is a disjuncture between your personal identity, which is both Black and white, and your social identity, which is Black; it takes some time and some doing to work it out for yourself."

It seems to me that such a burden carries with it possible privileges of vision and strength as well as possible disabilities of personal clarity. But you do have to work it out for yourself.

When my son was still an infant, a friend of mine invited me to join a freedom ride to Baltimore, Maryland. I had seen the burned and overturned buses of the freedom riders. I had seen the bleeding and bandaged heads of the freedom riders after white vigilanties attacked. And as I watched my son asleep in his crib, under the bluebird mobile, I resolved that I would go. To be sure, I was not remotely interested in traveling to Baltimore, but I thought, in the most literal-minded way, that my son might someday want to drink a cup of coffee while he drove through his country. I felt responsible for his future.

His father was furious: how could I risk my life like that? Didn't I care about what would happen to our son?

I went on that freedom ride as the wife of a white man and the mother of a Black child. None of it was easy. I was working out a disjuncture between my personal life and my social situation, for myself.

None of this means that any marriage is a great idea or a terrible thing. All I'm saying is that *love* is not the problem.

Black Folks on Nicaragua:
"Leave Those Folks Alone!"
October, 1983

I was talking with a Swiss agronomist in a northern co-operative near Somotillo. We stood on the rude earth of this new settlement to which some sixty refugee families had fled from the contras, three months before. As my cigarette neared the filter tip, I took it and tossed it to the ground, which I noticed, specifically, for the first time. The dirt was clean; nothing anywhere, but dirt and rocks. I bent to pick up the butt and put it in my pocket.

After a very long day traveling to the northern border and back, I returned to my hotel. On the floor of my room I saw a paper clip, and pounced upon it, later placing it carefully, alongside my tape-recording and camera gear. This is a very poor country.

The girl was singing this song:

> *see what the man have done (done)*
> *see how the red blood run (run)*

She was five. It was 7:30 a.m. in Pearl Lagoon, a small river community on the Atlantic coast of Nicaragua. She's Black and she speaks English. Including her beautiful bare feet, she was dressed for church. She moved to a reggae beat from her heart. She was singing because Miskito Indian refugees had arrived in Pearl Lagoon two nights earlier, fleeing contra murder and kidnappings executed in the middle of the night. I talked with Miskito women clearly still exhausted from their flight but, nonetheless, setting up huge pots of water for rice that the burning wood would slowly bring to a boil. One of the Miskitos, an infant, would not let her new friend, a tall Black woman, escape from her thin arms, even for a minute. "She's just a baby," the woman explained to me, laughing. "She thinks she's a baby!"

see what the man have done (done)
see how the red blood run (run)

When I interviewed Commandante Dora Maria Tellez, FSLN head of the Third Region of Nicaragua, which encompasses all of Managua and one-fifth of the total population, she exclaimed, "Do you realize that General Sandino (the nationalist hero of Nicaragua) was born exactly on the same day as Malcolm X, and not only that—he died on the same day and at the same age! Both were born the 18th of May," she raced ahead, "and both died on the 21st of February." Then, quietly: "I have a very special feeling for Malcolm."

Leaving an interview with Myriam Arguello, head of the opposition Conservative Democratic Party (PCD), in her Managua home, the young Nicaraguan interpreter with me grabbed my arm, her usual professional deadpan breaking down. "I can't believe Myriam Arguello said that to *you*!" she exclaimed, "telling you—a Black woman—that the PCD wants 'a democracy just like the one you have in the States'!" The translator could not control her laughter. "Oh God," she said, mortified and wiping away tears. "I can't believe she could be so stupid!" Arguello's comment became the funniest joke in town for a few days, as my translator repeated it to other Nicaraguans who invariably appreciated the punch line: "And do you know *who* she said this to? To *Chune*!! She said 'democracy' to a Black woman from America!"

In 1969, ten years before the Sandinista victory, the FSLN (Sandinista Front of National Liberation) published the thirteen articles of its program. This is Article XI, Section B: "It will support the struggle of the Black people and all the people of the United States for an authentic democracy and equal rights."

It is four years after the Sandinista revolution, and among the most resolute supporters of the Nicaraguan right to sovereign state integrity, among the most decisive, obdurate, and intellectually clear Americans concerned for the destiny of Central America, you will find the Black people of this country, from national levels of leadership straight to the pay phones on Harlem street corners.

Judy Simmons hosts a four-hour radio broadcast from WLIB in New York, five days a week. She has an audience of nearly 300,000 mostly Black listeners, daily, and she tells me that the consensus on Nicaragua is, "Leave those folks alone! Very definitely. There is a sense among my listeners that continental Africa, Central America, and the Caribbean are all linked through western exploitation. And this is articulated by my listeners who call in, consistently, and repeatedly. There is a felt assumption that people should have the right of self-determination—which is being abrogated in the Caribbean, denied in Central America, and denied in Southern Africa. They see this as analogous to our own situation, as Black people, here in the States."

Speaking for herself, and not as the moderator of the largest Black talk show in the country, Simmons adds emphatically, "I just resent and object to the Monroe Doctrine: that the only important thing is how the people who run the U.S. government and economy think. This is part and parcel of a perspective inimical to human rights, human dignity.

"As the Kerner Commission found out in the 60s," Simmons continues, "Black people are *really* disaffected from this country. So when they hear pronouncements coming from on high they're automatically skeptical: 'What are they up to now?!' Yes! There really is such a thing as a unified Black perspective. And right now the catchword is self-determination."

Black disaffection from American "democracy"—or Black realism, as I see it—may explain the extraordinary national Black opposition now working to interdict Reagan's Central America policies. The automatic skepticism that informs a healthy Black realism leads to the relative failure of official (and unofficial) sources of false information to saturate our households as thoroughly as the households of white Americans.

Manipulated news on the subject of Nicaragua, though, is so concerted, so energetic, so sonorously reiterated, that, by comparison, a U.S. aircraft carrier and seven destroyers idling off the coast of Nicaragua look like adolescent efforts at symbology. I went to Nicaragua, a Black realist exasperated by repeated reports that Nicaragua had been betrayed by the Sandinistas and that it had become a fascist state. I wanted to straighten out the stories and learn what lay behind Reagan's incessant allegations against Nicaragua. Some examples:

Nicaragua is exporting revolution. Nicaragua regularly sends significant military supplies to guerrillas in El Salvador.

There is, of course, no evidence. All the Nicaraguans I spoke with declared, absolutely, their support for the Salvadoran guerrilla movement—and absolutely denied sending them arms. The Reagan administration—failing to produce any evidence, ever—relies on the simplest disinformation tactic: the dogged repetition of a lie. Attempts by spokespeople to "explain" the charges often result in exchanges like this one, between U.S. Ambassador to Nicaragua Anthony Quainton and Jim Wallis, a reporter for the Christian magazine *Sojourners*:

Quainton: "We now know that massive amounts of arms are going from Nicaragua to El Salvador across the Gulf of Fonseca by dugout canoe."

Wallis: "*Massive* amounts? By canoe?"

Quainton: "Well, substantial amounts."

Wallis: "Do you have any documentation? There must be evidence—the U.S. has a lot of sophisticated surveillance equipment here."

Quainton: "Well, no. We don't have photographs. The canoes are too small to be detected by our satellites."

Nicaragua has broken its contract with the OAS; Nicaragua has refused to hold elections.

The only resolution the OAS ever made about Nicaragua was entered into June 1979, before the Sandinistas came to power. It condemned Somoza.

As for elections: the Sandinistas have never deviated from their promise to hold elections six years after their victory, pointing out that it took the United States more than twice as long to hold elections after the American Revolution.

As for elections: I witnessed noisy debate in the Council of State, where representatives of more than nine different political parties were drafting laws for the 1985 national elections. Furthermore, three months later, I read the *New York Times* report on national conventions and rallies by opposition political parties preparing, under Nicaraguan election law, to "aspire to power" without restriction.

And as for elections: tell Mississippi Black folks about elections.

Cuba and the Soviet Union control Nicaragua: they have turned it into an aggressive military power that threatens our security.

I did meet Cubans in Nicaragua. There are Cuban medical volunteers, training and treating Nicaraguans. The first Cuban I met, however, was there to teach pre-school gymnastics. The only other Cuban with whom I spoke at length was an artist. I also met Swedes in Nicaragua, German nurses, French doctors, Dutch journalists, a Mexican nun, and one other Black American: all internationalist volunteers. I did not meet anyone, from Cuba or anywhere else, who would try "running" what has to be the most fiercely nationalistic revolution imaginable. Nicaragua, after a century of control by U.S. mining, banking, and fruit companies backed by the marines, is finally being run by Nicaraguans.

As for the military threat posed by Nicaragua: Nicaragua has never invaded the territory of any country, despite regular transgressions of its own boundaries by enemies of the Sandinista regime. And finally, disinformation from the Democrats: Reagan is leading the United States into a war with Nicaragua. What would you call it if 600 white Americans had been killed so far this year by invaders at our northern border?

The United States is already at war with Nicaragua.

North American freedom of the press generally denies Black people due voice and due coverage of our efforts to solidify our voices into representative government programs and postures. Particularly in the realm of foreign policy, Black folks should remember their place—their domestic place. *Time* magazine, in a cover story on Black political power, profiled U.S. Representative Mickey Leland with clear bewilderment: "He speaks out on global politics." Despite the widespread notion that it is reasonable only for white congressmen to take an interest in global politics, an historic, brave, and possibly determining number of national Black leaders have seen "what the man have done" in Central America, and don't like it.

This response arises out of our history. Angela Gilliam, the anthropologist, writes in the Fall, 1983 issue of *Freedomways*:

> The principled outspokenness displayed by Martin Luther King, Jr. and Malcolm X, and earlier by W.E.B. DuBois and Paul Robeson, set the tone for the black community to become more and more deeply involved in international affairs...such involvement is not only natural and proper but imperative, because the international is more and more tied in with the domestic, all of humanity's condition more and more tied in with each individual's condition.

Rational identification with the First World transforms us—Black folks—from a minority into members of the world's majority, and this means power. This means, for example, that what we are doing now may actually stop the blood run in Central America.

Ronald V. Dellums, the U.S. Representative from the 8th District, California, said on November 30, 1982:

It is sobering to consider the extent of the human suffering that is the lot of the ordinary Nicaraguans living and working in the border areas—murder, kidnapping, rape, torture, and mutilation are almost common place occurrences. Shamefully, the beasts who commit these atrocities are agents of the United States government.

I cannot stand by without asserting the fundamental principle which it is my role in this case to raise—that it is not the constitutional right or duty of the president to declare war, secretly or otherwise.[1]

Ron Dellums is suing the president of the United States. The case he refers to is *Sanchez v. Reagan,* filed November 30, 1982, by attorneys at the Center for Constitutional Rights, a public interest civil rights law firm, and the National Lawyers Guild. Dellums joined seven Nicaraguan citizens, victims of contra attacks, and two Florida residents seeking to close down contra training camps in Dade County, as plaintiffs against defendants Ronald Reagan, and other top administration officials. Charging the defendants with criminal violation of domestic and international law, the suit demanded damages for the plaintiffs and injunctive relief against further contra attacks. On July 19, 1983, *Sanchez v. Reagan* was amended to include additional plaintiffs—among them, nine more members of the Congressional Black Caucus.

Sanchez v. Reagan charges the defendants with violation of the Neutrality Act (which prohibits aid to groups attacking a country with which the United States is at peace), the Boland Amendment (which prohibits aid to groups seeking to overthrow the Nicaraguan government), and the United States Constitution, which gives only Congress the right to wage war. And, say the lawyers, "This is an international police brutality case...designed to question whether American foreign policy may with impunity be carried out by means which violate the most basic and universally recognized human rights."[2]

One of the defendants, Thomas Enders, then assistant secretary of state for Latin American Affairs, admitted that the United States was "winking" at violations of the Neutrality Act. And national media made the term "secret war" ludicrous, as daily revelations about U.S. support for the contras leaked out, and Reagan praised "freedom fighters" against the Nicaraguan government. Nonetheless, on August 1, 1983, a federal judge dismissed *Sanchez v. Reagan*, asserting that it was a "political" case and, therefore, nonjusticiable.

Michael Ratner, attorney at the Center for Constitutional Rights, has announced that an appeal will follow, directly: "The federal defendants essentially assume that they can act in a totally lawless manner," he says. "But Congress has passed laws, and the courts must enforce them. These are war crimes and war criminals!"[3]

So *Sanchez v. Reagan* moves into appeal, joining another CCR lawsuit brought by Black congressman George Crockett against Ronald Reagan, challenging U.S. policy in El Salvador through the War Powers Resolution. At this moment the right of the president to wage war is a question under serious re-examination in Congress and in the press, not only with respect to Central America, but also to Lebanon. These Black congress members, therefore, not only "speak out on global politics," but they are leading domestic efforts to properly solve the historical problem of a president's discretionary powers.

Members of the Black Caucus do not appear particularly affected by the opposition to their opposition: eleven of the twenty-nine plaintiffs in *Crockett v. Reagan* are Black, among them Harold Washington, George Crockett, Ronald Dellums, William Clay, Melvyn Dymally, Walter Fauntroy, Mickey Leland, Gus Savage, Parren Mitchell, and Major Owens—all plaintiffs in both suits. The Black Caucus does not seem to share Democratic timidity about Central America.

Major Owens recently held a special town meeting on Central America in his Brooklyn District. Responding with a sense of urgency, his constituents packed the meeting. "It's their concern," says Owens, "that the issue of Central America and specifically Nicaragua threaten to embroil the whole Caribbean in a cold war—if not a hot one!"[4]

"It's my highest priority," declares Mickey Leland from Texas. "It should be everyone's priority, what the president's doing in Nicaragua. The president is trying to talk us into war."[5]

Congressman George Crockett analyzed the Black response when I spoke with him, underscoring his colleagues' concerns. "In general," he says, "Blacks would be opposed to the kind of waste you see when money's being thrown away on military relief for despotic, corrupt regimes like the one in El Salvador. But it's more. On the part of this administration we see the tendency to side with whites whenever there's a conflict between whites and non-whites. Or, in Central America and the Caribbean, where you have a class basis of power, to side with those at the top who play ball with the imperial interests that dominate those economies."

Crockett pauses, but briefly: "I think you'd be hard put to find any Black leader here who has not expressed opposition to Reagan's Central America policies. There's a direct link between Reagan's policies there and Reagan's policies in this country that affect Black people."

To test this assertion, I put a call through to Jesse Jackson's PUSH headquarters. His office sent me a statement Jackson had just released, appealing to the American people "to recall their own revolutionary past...to renounce and reject the policies of interference in the internal affairs of Central America, and the military intervention and national arrogance that have too often made us a partner in the exploitation and oppression of our American neighbors." Jackson, who was rumored to be about to declare his candidacy for president, described as "untenable" the prospect of "poor Blacks and Hispanics...of the United States being asked to fight against their poor Black and brown brothers and sisters in Central America."

And Ronald Dellums, still determined, has filed yet another lawsuit, this time against Attorney General William Smith. Smith refused to investigate Dellums' charge of criminal behavior by administration officials against Nicaragua. Under the Ethics in Government Act, Dellums is suing to have a special prosecutor undertake the investigation.

Neither Dellums nor Crockett nor their brothers in Congress and the national Black leadership seem to get weary. They seem to get stronger, or as the poet Sterling Brown has written, "The strong men keep on comin'." Even as in the 1960s where the first arena for Black power was the courtroom, the law is now on trial. *Ubi jus ibi remedium* (where there is a law there must be a remedy): strong men are again testing this concept.

But it is not the law, it is the meaning of the crime, that Black people everywhere recognize and that motivates the calls to Judy Simmons's radio show:

*"Where were the Marines and the training bases when Russia took Afghanistan or Poland? They never fight each other. They'll fight Vietnam, Korea, and...now they gonna fight Nicaragua and all down there where the people can't bomb them back."

*"This bit about overt debate on covert action to overthrow other people's government really takes me out!"

*"If we [Black people] got more serious about South Africa, we would have to come together on El Salvador, Grenada, and Nicaragua."

We have heard the United States' allegations against small people before, in other bellicose campaigns. We have seen state violence before, as now we see U.S. military violence poised against Nicaragua. (Wasn't it Black children who led the struggle and faced the dogs and nightsticks in Selma, just as fourteen year old Sandinistas faced down tanks supplied by the U.S.?) We recognize the criminals: George Schultz, boasting as he holds a gun to the heads of the Nicaraguan people that "It's working!"

It is not working. It is not making us or the Nicaraguan men and women or any First World peoples love that gun or love the hand that holds it to our heads. It is not making us weak. It is not making us stop making up our own minds to live our own lives, or die.

"Patria Libre o Muerte," say the Nicaraguan people. And they mean that. And so, increasingly, do we.

We have seen how the red blood run (run)
We have seen what the man have done (done)

Chapter 9

Nicaragua:
Why I had to Go There
January, 1984

Like a lot of Black women, I have always had to invent the power my freedom requires:

All my life I've been studying revolution. I've been looking for it, pushing at the possibilities and waiting for that moment when there's no more room for rhetoric, for research or for reason: when there's only my life or my death left to act upon. Here in the United States you do get weary, after a while; you could spend your best energies forever writing letters to the *New York Times*. But you know, in your gut, that writing back is not the same as fighting back.

I know that the end of the 20th century will finally belong to the majority—the First World peoples of the earth who look like you and me—or there will be no one left on the planet. This argument between the rich and the poor is just that serious. I know that the global lunging of First World peoples into power is everywhere opposed by a North American "foreign policy" that depends, entirely, on my inertia and my tax money.

I had to go to Nicaragua. That Central American country of 2.7 million people, that place as small as the state of Iowa, that front-page First World nation with a population spread as meagerly as what you'd find in the Sahara desert: that home of Indian/African/Spanish women and men mostly doing without running water and electricity. That "threat" to "national security," that "backyard"/"frontyard" monster of "Marxism-Leninism" repeatedly conjured up by the White House cowboy as "the menace" to "our credibility" around the world. Why is he so hot and bothered? What is making the big guys lose their usual but deadly, cool?

Back in 1979, when the Sandinistas overthrew "the world's greediest" dictator, Somoza, I knew this revolution would be different. Although the people of Nicaragua had suffered a saturation level of atrocities during Somoza's rule, after the victory there were no mass executions. The Sandinistas pardoned their enemies and abolished the death penalty. Rather than one man, a junta of nine leaders—including one woman—took control, and everybody running the new government looked like kids: they were young people. (Not "young" as in "the young John F. Kennedy, forty-four years old," but nineteen or twenty years old.) And, exactly one day after the Sandinista triumph of July 19, 1979, these "kids" passed a law prohibiting prostitution and also prohibiting the exploitation of women in any and all advertising. On top of these peculiarities, many of the revolutionaries of Nicaragua were poets.

I had to go there.

Early in 1983 I had been invited to Nicaragua, as a poet, by the poet Roberto Vargas, First Secretary of Cultural Affairs at the Nicaraguan Embassy in Washington, D.C. He wanted me to read my poetry to the people there. He told me about the 27,000 Black Nicaraguans living on the Atlantic coast of the country. For them, English is a first language. Also fluent in Spanish, they are fully bilingual citizens who reached those shores in one of three ways: as survivors of an early 19th century slave ship mutiny, as runaway slaves from Jamaica/Barbados/Grenada or as laborers imported by British colonialists who attempted to settle this east coast of Nicaragua in 1894.

But by the time of Roberto's invitation, the U.S. press had revealed that Reagan had committed $19 million in CIA funds to recruit, feed and arm opponents of the revolution (called *contras*). And the State Department was busily wheezing out lies intended to discredit the Sandinistas and mislead the U.S. public. In such circumstances, poetry might be quite beside the point, which was really to save the revolution from this escalation of hostilities and terror. Armed and goaded by the CIA, *contra* troops based in Honduras daily invaded Nicaraguan border towns: blowing up bridges/burning hospitals/ambushing international press personnel/murdering doctors/blowing up babies and tobacco barns.

I wanted to see for myself what was happening. I wanted to face the violence reported by the newspapers and supported by my taxes: to make my witness to this First World dream before it buckled into yet another nightmare colony, another "vacation paradise," another "vital" outpost of the big guys. I wanted to get real: to put my life, as well as my words, on the line. I had to go to Nicaragua.

On a sunny Friday afternoon at 5:15, as the attendant on my Aeronica flight announced, "Ladies and gentlemen, we are now beginning our descent into the free territory of Nicaragua." I looked below the clouds beneath the plane for Managua, by far the largest city and, by our North American standards, the only "city" of Nicaragua. But there was nothing to see: rock; mountain; patches of scrubgrass; no roads; nothing. Oh, maybe that was a road! But nothing on either side of it, and nothing on it. I saw miles and miles of farmland, but no houses. As we cut the treetops to land, I saw one or two cows grazing to my left.

Where the hell are the "Soviet missiles"? I asked myself. *Where would you "hide" them?* And, more urgently, *Where was I? Where was Nicaragua?*

During the ride to the hotel, I see, here, tin-roofed shacks reminiscent of mountain parishes in Jamaica; there, an open stream running into the mud. I see children with no shoes and shirts with no buttons. I see banana trees with large leaves that, compared with the rickety squalor of the shacks, look luxurious and certainly sheltering. It is so hot and so steamy that my eyeglasses become useless by the time I take a second step outside. But I leave my hotel, easily cross the four-lane thoroughfare. (There is almost no traffic in either direction. There may be a bus going by and then, late, a truck, and perhaps, afterward, a taxi; but mostly there is silence.) I feel like a giant as I peer down the mudslide leading from the highway to the barrio where 100 families live in a swept dirt compound. Tin roofs top the lean-to huts patched together with scrap wood. These homes have no windows, and there are no doors. Outside, the "kitchen" is an old table, a pail of water from the barrio well and a standing fire that serves as the stove. All the people I see are colored people— tan/brown/black—and as small (five feet, three inches) or smaller than I am. It's so hot I would do anything for a cup of water.

As I walk along, it hits me that I have never seen such hovel levels of struggle for daily life. Or such cleanliness and order and quiet. The dirt is kept clean by homemade brooms. The hair is combed. I hear no shouts, no babies screaming.

Nowhere in the South, nowhere in Jamaica or Puerto Rico, nowhere have I seen anything like this combination of no shoes

and no floor, inside apparently half-deserted, but utterly organized, space. Where is everybody? *Where is everybody? This is the
capital city!*

Unless you are careful, you might conclude that Nicaragua is
nowhere and that nobody lives there, and so, why not do whatever
might cross your imperial mind?

But Nicaragua is more than anybody's idea about the place.
It's real. Its people seem to think they have rights to their own
land, and their own leaders. It's a bad example. If other First
World people, if we, ourselves, took a notion to think and act just
according to what we felt was good for us, if we thought and if we
acted as though the big guys should just take a flying jump out of
the nearest window whenever they come pushing their craziness
into our countries, our houses, our heads, the whole world would
soon become really different really fast. The big guys would lose
control, and the next thing you know, most of us would find
ourselves in the middle of a revolution based on self-respect.
Nicaragua is a bad example. It's little David, with his mouth
making up a catchy song about freedom—it's little David, standing up to Goliath on his bare feet. It's a very bad example.

Most of the people of the world walk around on bare feet while
the eagles fly over the globe, looking for lunch: "Pass me the salt?"

"Sure. Pass me Brazil."

"You should try a little of this Angola over here."

"Well, actually, I thought I'd order some Grenada. (Or Lebanon. Or Chad. Or Guatemala.) Just something to kill my appetite."

These days, when the eagle wants something for lunch, he
usually screams, "Communists!" or "Cuba!" or "National security!" In the old days, however, he used to solemnly say "gold" or
"slaves" or "Civilization," and then these words would produce a
great bustling of imperial energies, as newly marked areas of the
map became targets for conquest and imperial exploitation.

Bounded by the Pacific Ocean on the west and the Caribbean
on the east, Nicaragua does not qualify as a gold mine, or an oil
field, or a treasury of diamonds. But there is more than enough
arable land to feed its people—if there were roads and trucks and
tractors and parts for tractors when they break down; and if
peasant farmers and their families were not being killed or
kidnapped and tortured by counterrevolutionary commandos (the
contras) based in Honduras and recruited, trained and paid by the
United States to "destabilize" the Nicaraguan government.

By the time of the American Civil War in the 1860s, the U.S. had intervened in Nicaragua three times. The eagle thought that Nicaragua's southern border—one of the narrowest stretches of land in Central America—would make a swell place for a canal. As the U.S. Ambassador to Nicaragua, William Merry, pointed out in 1890, "The nation that controls Nicaragua will control the destiny of the Western Hemisphere." The marines came again and again, looking for lunch, occupying Nicaragua, in the words of President Calvin Coolidge, "in order to protect American property."

In 1933, Nicaragua's national hero, Augusto Cesar Sandino, and his guerrilla army of peasants and farmers forced the marines out. *Patria libre o muerte,"* said Sandino. "Free country or death!"

But to replace the departing marines, the United States invented a new police force—the National Guard—and appointed Anastasio Somoza Garcia, a Nicaraguan trained in U.S. military schools, as its head. Somoza assassinated Sandino, elevated himself to "president" of the country and began a family dynasty that ruled through horrifying force until 1979. In the first four years of his rule, for example, Somoza's personal wealth increased by $4 million. The average yearly wage of a Nicaraguan citizen for the same period was $11. Somoza controlled Nicaragua totally, through the National Guard. No one was safe from their terror tactics. Slashing breasts, pulling out fingernails, gouging out eyes, raping women and girls, kidnapping children, burning bodies, mutilating prisoners, the Guard became legendary for its uncontrolled sadism. As resistance to this savage repression grew, the Guard conducted aerial bombardment of Nicaragua's cities, using napalm, mortars and machine guns in an all-out war against its own people.

During the nearly half-century of Somoza's dictatorship, U.S. financial and political interests flourished there without restraint. "He may be a sonofabitch," said President Theodore Roosevelt about Somoza, "but he's *our* sonofabitch."

The Somoza family, described in 1975 by the *Washington Post* as "the world's greediest dictatorship," seized more than half of all the private property in Nicaragua, 30% of the arable farmlands and controlling interest in every remaining national resource— from radio and tv stations to railroads and factories. Somoza and the sons who succeeded him received billions of aid dollars from the United States. Even the Red Cross relief found its way into the family coffers after the 1972 earthquake destroyed Managua.

But the people prevailed. Led by the FSLN (the Sandinista Front for National Liberation), the women, the men, the eleven and twelve year old Sandinista fighters of Nicaragua defeated the dictatorship that had terrorized and depleted their national life for forty-seven years.

On July 19, 1979, the Sandinista revolution triumphed: Somoza escaped to the United States, leaving behind him 50,000 dead, a $1.6 billion foreign debt and $0.25 the national coffers. Country-wide illiteracy ran higher than 85%, polio was rampant, and diseases such as measles were everywhere fatal to children already suffering from malnutrition.

The Sandinista victory was more than a revolt against the unbearable: it was an altogether conscious movement toward a fully conceived vision of another a better way to live.

Four years later, when I went to Nicaragua, I found the revolution very much in progress. An astounding literacy campaign conducted by 80,000 volunteers (the majority women and teenagers) had reduced illiteracy to less than 12%. I saw families living in new cooperatives and learned that the Sandinista government has given land titles to more than 125,000 peasant families. I found health care available for free or else for $0.10 a visit—depending on the ability to pay—and learned that polio had been eradicated and that massive immunization campaigns had been completed nationwide. I discovered that university enrollment had doubled, with tuition at $2 a semester, that primary education was free and that 70% of all Nicaraguans, children and adults, were enrolled in some kind of educational program.

I saw women working alongside men, confident that the new laws that mandated equal pay for equal work, and that recognized the value of housework as well, would protect the quality of their labor and wages. The revolution—and the role of women in bringing it about—has meant real changes in a country where even now 60% of all families are headed by single women. Through AMNLAE (the National Women's Organization, named for the first women to die fighting with the FSLN), women have succeeded in establishing laws that enforce child-support payments by absent fathers and that formally establish legal and economic justice for women.

I went everywhere I could, and everywhere I went I saw the motto: All arms to the people. I saw all of the people armed: nine year olds, Black women, elderly men. Everyone was armed with World War II rifles or AK-47's or whatever might come to hand;

people forming volunteer militia to defend the revolution they had made.

It's Tuesday: I am preparing to leave Bluefields, the major "city" of the east coast, population 23,000. The mayor is a Black man, the regional governor is a Black man and the people are Black—Afro-Caribbeans as they call themselves. Identifying strongly with other Afro-Caribbean communities, the music of these Nicaraguans is reggae, and the cooking base coconut oil. These Nicaraguans can easily eat shrimp, lobster or fish three meals a day. The main industry is fishing. Because neither the British colonialists nor Somoza bothered to construct roads or other elementary communication networks—especially in this part of the country—the primary mode of transportation is still boat, or more precisely, dugout canoe.

"We are a river people," Francisco Campbell proudly explains. He is the tall and handsome Black man who serves as First Secretary of Political Affairs in the Nicaraguan Embassy in Washington D.C. "Since the Sandinista Revolution," Francisco tells me, "the government has created special university scholarships for Afro-Caribbean students. These scholarships cover tuition, housing, food and all the high cost of travel to and from Leon [the Pacific coast city where Nicaragua's university is located]." Francisco's brother Enrique Campbell, was the first and only geophysicist of Nicaragua. He was killed by U.S. backed *contras* in December, 1982.

It's indescribably hot, easily 115 degrees. I am traveling with three other North American activists and our guide/translator. The people of Bluefields cannot stop showing their gratitude that we have come among them, that we have volunteered to share the danger of their lives for a couple of days. They have convened a sudden street festival in our honor, held on the first, new basketball court where they dance for us and where I am introduced with embarrassing fuss and praise and asked to read my poetry. They present me with handcrafted gifts and homemade record albums of Bluefields reggae. They throw parties where the rum and the dancing and the live music leave me delirious and sleepy, all at once. They hug and kiss us incessantly.

The eagerness of their gentle affection makes me self-conscious: I take care not to seem, even for a minute, uncomfortable. But I am all of these things. The notorious energy of the Sandinistas has begun to exhaust my own. Steadily following a schedule of eighteen to twenty hours a day of interviews, travel

We talk until the dawn. He comes from Esteli, a town north of Managua. He is "far from home." He writes poetry, but "not for work." He wants to know how the people of the United States opposed to the aggression against Nicaragua are organized. He wonders if I imagined I would sleep on the stone bench of a park when I planned my trip here. He wants to know what do I do, and about my son: How old is he, and what does he do? He thinks that tonight is a poem of my sleeping in the park and then our talking with each other. We speak only in Spanish; when I do not understand he slowly repeats himself, in Spanish, until I do understand.

At 5:00 a.m. he suggests that I follow him into the police station; it may be warmer there. Inside the station, he cermoniously places a white wicker rocking chair in the center of an otherwise bare room, and asks me to sit in it, and rest myself.

Even now I can hear Faustino: talking to me, softly, close to the ending of the night.

I think about the land of Goliath, where I come from. I know he is as serious as snakebite about his very bad example. If he cannot act the bully and get away with it, in a country so small and so poor as Nicaragua, then Goliath will have to do something truly new: earn friendships and recognize First World peoples as fully legitimate, fully equal human beings to be reckoned with.

That would mean an absolute reversal of North American habits in the context of the world. That would mean the end of North American power imposed by force, the one superiority Reagan and company can presume, at the moment. And even though it's clear that the U.S. will "conquer" Nicaragua only by erasing it from the earth, entirely, I am hardly reassured. Reagan may very well choose to do that, to try to efface this terrible example from our consciousness. The stakes are that high.

This will mean war/more war. This will mean disproportionately high numbers of Black men on the target line, as foot soldiers—in the chumpseat of evil maneuvers—against people who look like you and me, people who want only what we want: to escape the hatred, and the tyranny of those who are stronger and richer than we; to live through our own dreams. To be free.

War will further reduce even such lunatic obscenities as Reagan's cheese for the hungry and smiling good cheer for the desperately unemployed. War will mean death on an unpredictable/uncontrollable scale, if we do not force Reagan back into and under sane and humane control.

Where will that leave us? I think that will leave us where we are, right now: kneeling to a man who hates the sight of our face. I think that will leave us ashamed, begging and ashamed.

As I make my way home, my head throbs with Nicaragua: how very green it is. How many different ways it seems good and growing, everywhere. How easily the people laugh. How the heat never stops, even at night; how it stays hot so that you lust for anything to drink. How hard it is to boil water when first you must find the water and then you must find the wood for the fire.

How many of these gentle people have I helped to kill just by paying my taxes? How could these people living in this poor country where so many dreams arise from the facts of so much horror, how could they ever hurt me or ever hurt any of us, up here, in the chill indifference of North America?

They have given to me and to all of us an amazing example of self-love. With their bodies and their blood they have shown us the bravery that self-love requires. They persist. The new laws and the new programs integral to their new life persist. And the enemies of this truly progressive First World revolution persist.

And what will I, what will we, give to them in return? What will we do about these enemies of the new life that each of us needs? *Will we be quick enough?*

Compared with barefoot David standing up to Goliath, we, Black Americans, are so very rich and so very powerful. But when will we believe it? When will we emulate the spirit of the visions of the Sandinistas? *When will we seize the world around us with our freedom?*

Chapter 10

Life After Lebanon
October, 1984

Let me just say, at once: I am not now nor have I ever been a whiteman. And, leaving aside the joys of unearned privilege, this leaves me feeling pretty good: I am glad I am not the whiteman who warns that Nicaragua is next on his evil list and who, meanwhile, starves and terrorizes that country through "covert action." I am glad I am not the whiteman who congratulates El Salvador and who supports South Africa. I am glad I am not the whiteman who lies about Managua and who denies asylum to real freedom fighters opposed to Pretoria. I am glad I am not the whiteman who dyes his hair, wears pancake makeup, and then tries to act like the last cowboy out here surrounded by wild Indians. I am glad I am not the whiteman whose poor little helpmeet used to sleep beside him with a pistol (albeit an expensive, delicate, and ladylike pistol) under her pillow. I am glad I am not the whiteman whose wife publicly saw fit to call another woman *a bitch*. Or, more precisely, to call another woman a term rhyming with *rich*. (Evidently this means that the language of the latrine becomes acceptable and, better yet, properly female, if you intimate and euphemize your infamies.) I am glad I am not the whiteman who thinks it's Old Boy Manly to describe his debate with the Democratic candidate for Vice President of the United States as "kicking a little ass." I am glad I am not the whiteman who advised Geraldine Ferrarro to pretend she's actually another whiteman: to look dull, act calm, or to just generally let the lies and insults roll, without appropriate, emotional, and justified retaliation. I am very glad that I am not a single one of the several, very powerful whitemen who, in their American manliness, have failed, outstandingly failed, to defend Geraldine Ferrarro from unjust, undue, and obnoxious harrassment, such as not one of them has ever had to confront:[1] What do you suppose would happen if a Soviet leader, after meeting with Ronald Reagan, and after returning to Moscow, reported in this fashion on those talks: "Oh well, I kicked a little ass."?

I see all of this as what I will summarize as The New Manliness. Craven and cowardly by its nature, these North American machos absolutely abhor the fair fight, the face to face argument between equals and, instead, preoccupy themselves with a relentless assault upon those who are indisputably smaller and weaker than they. In the world of these New Men, you do not turn to Daddy when you need help because Daddy's busy beating up Mommy and, if he notices you standing around, he may very well hurl your nine-year-old torso against the dining room wall. These New Men follow a rather cross-eyed vision of Far West mythology. No longer does The New Man pit himself against much greater odds than he can ever see—pestilence, drought, outlaw bands of cattle thieves, and corporate encroachment upon his lands. Instead, he preys upon his wife, his children, his Black co-worker, the poor, the elderly, Grenada, Nicaragua, and he boasts about it—if not at the neighborhood bar, then at a full scale press conference held at The Big House.

When I refer to the New Man, I am not speaking about someone with natural tendencies to batter or oppress. I do not mean that all whitemen are reducible to their color or their gender. The New Man is someone who maintains a system of unequal power relations in order to preserve his own domination. And he is willing to do this at any cost. This is why a woman is battered every fifteen seconds in this country, and this is why Geraldine Ferrarro has been the target for unprecedented, unequal abuse, and this is why every developing nation on the planet must sweat to secure its sovereign rights of independent ways and means away from the depradations of these New Men in the poisonous bloom of their New Manliness. This is why Jesse Jackson, unarguably the presidential candidate with the least resources available to him, was the candidate most vilified, most ridiculed and, despite his having delivered six million new registered voters to the Democratic Party, was the most abandoned by the leaders of the Democrats, and the most humiliated by the Democrats who have rejected everything and everyone he, Jesse Jackson, so eloquently represented. And, like Geraldine Ferrarro, the Reverend Jesse Jackson has been bullied into gestures conciliatory towards his enemies;

his enemies have pushed him into postures that none of them would ever think to adopt: Who has demanded that Ronald Reagan repudiate Jerry Falwell or Jesse Helms?[2] When have you ever seen Ronald Reagan or Walter Mondale ask the people of this country to forgive him? And can you recall any whiteman, can you imagine any whiteman, ever saying to you, "Be patient with me; God has not finished with me yet"?[3]

And yet, on record, what are the crimes of Jesse Jackson, for which he should ask forgiveness? Show me the dead, the hungry, the desolate, the subverted, the bombed out, the burned up; show me evidence of his wrong-doing. Who is the whiteman, anywhere, to whom the Reverend Jackson should apologize?

This cross-eyed New Manliness of North America explains why the ostensible great threat is another Big Guy, the Soviet Union, and yet it is not the Big Guy's actual property that the United States will invade, it is not Soviet waters that the United States will mine. It is some other country, some small, some weak, some non-white country allegedly under Soviet influence that The New Men of the USA will choose to torture and destroy—rather than face another whiteman who just might kick his ass, a little bit. The New Men of the USA madly develop abstract systems for nuclear annihilation because that will mean that at least they didn't "lose" simply because nobody can win that showdown.

So I am glad, I am truly glad that I am not now, nor have I ever been, a whiteman.

But where does all of this happiness, this relief, put me, exactly?

I must think about the woman who was interviewed on TV, immediately following the Bush-Ferrarro debate. She said she would vote for Reagan because she would feel "safe" with a man. Like George Bush. And I cannot overlook the woman quoted in today's press; she said she felt good about Geraldine because Geraldine "stayed calm."

Given the near-hysterical nastiness of much of what came out of his mouth, given the obvious misogyny and the scorn that determined his behavior towards his opponent, and given the merciless and warmongering policies of his administration to date, I must conclude that that woman would feel safe only because George Bush is not a woman. She knows that no woman is safe in this man's world, and that no woman, so far, has been able to create and assure safety for herself, and other women, in this man's world. She spoke, in other words, from the desperation that a realistic understanding of gender politics will yield. But she was speaking against the one instance in our history, the instance of Geraldine Ferrarro, when a woman might accede to a position of enough power so that she could begin to design and establish safety for herself, and for other women. That woman who spoke against Geraldine Ferrarro, hers was a failure of faith tantamount to capitulation: However understandable, hers was an act of self-hatred.

The other woman, the one who seemed pleased by Ferrarro's staying "calm" seems to me related: Unless you accept white male standards of conduct, standards that castigate women for our "emotionality," our tears, our tendencies to take human life and responsible love quite seriously, why would you applaud any woman for remaining "calm" in an outrageous circumstance? What would be the reason to fault Ferrarro for becoming furious, indignant, disgusted, and thoroughly impassioned, as she right-eously reacted to the lies and the self-absorbed and morbid and patronizing complacencies of Mr. George Bush?

But while I must think of these two women, and I must wonder when they will ever identify self-respect as a reasonable goal that we can join together to approach, there are many, many other women, in this country, and around the world, who are not now, nor have they ever been whitemen: Women who are making over this place of ours into a place of safety for all of us, including white men.

The values and the methods of these women, women com-pletely uninterested in keeping calm, women entirely prepared to make a scene, to raise a ruckus and to be shrill, if you will, these women I may describe to you as New Women.

Two years ago it was a Jewish woman who first alerted me to the Israeli invasion of Lebanon, and to the issues of that horren-dous episode in our history: territorial integrity, the survival of the Palestinian people, facts versus propaganda, self-determination versus neocolonialism, and American taxes—my and your mon-ey—providing the Israeli armed forces with means to carry out this invasion of another country.

It was an Israeli woman who informed me about the Peace Now movement inside Israel, a movement opposed to the inva-sion, and opposed to the massacre of the Palestinian people. It was an Israeli woman who warned me that the ulterior purpose of the invasion was Israeli settlement of the West Bank, i.e. complete displacement and disenfranchisement of the Palestinian people.

During the summer of 1982, it was another Jewish woman with whom I spoke daily, comparing newspaper and radio accounts, tracking eyewitnesses recently returned from Lebanon, and planning whatever we could to counter the lies that saturated the U.S. media; we wanted to stop the war. The other people with whom I kept my witness, and wept, and worked, that summer, were, again, mostly women, and mostly Jewish women. For a long time I believe that we supposed the problem was that of misinformation. If only Americans knew the truth of things then they would rally to help, to stop the invasion, the slaughter.

What I gradually began to understand, however, was something importantly different. The problem was not one of misinformation, or ignorance. The problem was that the Lebanese people, in general, and that the Palestinian people, in particular, are not whitemen: They never have been whitemen. Hence they were and they are only Arabs, or terrorists, or animals. Certainly they were not men and women and children; certainly they were not human beings with rights remotely comparable to the rights of whitemen, the rights of a nation of whitemen.

In addition, I learned as a result of a poem I wrote that was published in July 1982, in *The Village Voice*, and I learned as a result of all of the op-ed pieces of mine that the *New York Times* unabashedly refused to print, that no women and that certainly no non-white woman should presume to think about/form an opinion/construct an analysis of any issue of conflict between any whitemen. Either the whitemen in this country will censor and block the publication of such a woman's thoughts, or they will whitelist and pounce upon her with such epithets as "anti-Semitic" and "naive" and "divisive."

In the fall of 1982, myself and two other women met at my house to discuss what else we might attempt. This was immediately prior to the massacre of Sabra and Shatilah. We decided to convene a poetry reading in which North American poets, Israeli poets, and Arab poets would combine their poetry inside an event to benefit the children of Lebanon: All monies raised by the reading would go directly to UNICEF, for the maimed and homeless children victimized by the invasion. After much toil the other two women, both of them young white poets, and one of them Jewish, succeeded in organizing an historic poetry reading in which, indeed, Israeli, Arab, and American poets literally agreed to appear on the same stage on the same night.

As it happens, I was the last poet to read, that evening. When I finished, I found myself surrounded by large whitemen, two of them Israeli poets, all of them yelling at me and threatening me with the looming bulk of their bodies.

It was women who got me out of that auditorium.

It was women, one of them Black, one of them Jewish, one of them WASP, who watched out for me, and who "covered my back" at the reception following, a reception at which one whiteman told a young Jewish woman that I, "That Black woman over there should be burned alive in green fire."

It is noteworthy that this particular whiteman did not say this directly to me. Nor did he address his vile remarks to my son who was standing not more than three feet away from him, and who would have cheerfully punched out his lights, so to speak. It is noteworthy that not one white man, Israeli or otherwise, said anything to me, directly, except when he stood as part of a group of whitemen hugely outnumbering me.

But what I find more memorable are the women of that summer and of that November evening, 1982: The New Women of the New Womanliness who persisted against the male white rhetoric about *borders* and *national security* and *terrorism* and *democracy* and *vital interests*. And I also find memorable the distinguished U.S. Congressman, John Conyers, who nobly em-ceed that benefit poetry reading, and who hosted the reception afterwards: John Conyers is not now, nor has he ever been, a whiteman.

The Israeli invasion of Lebanon, the complicity of Americans through tax monies that supported the invasion, the slaughter of Lebanese peoples, the decimation and rout of the Palestinian peoples, the awesome determination by whitemen, in this country, to silence or to discredit American dissent, the vicious wielding about of the term anti-Semitic whenever anyone protested the interminable carnage executed and precipitated by that invasion, left me extremely embittered, shocked, and wondering about life after Lebanon: What would that be like?

In fact, the intellectual community, including the feminist community of North America, and the entire community of the political left in America separated into two seemingly irreconcilable groups, at a minimum: There were those for whom Israel remained a sacrosanct subject exempt from rational discussion and dispute, and there were those to whom Israel looked a whole lot like yet another country run by whitemen whose militarism tended to produce racist consequences; i.e. the disenfranchisement and subjugation of non-white peoples, peoples not nearly as strong as they.

Now it is one thing to disagree and quite another to prohibit disagreement. The invasion of Lebanon erected a subject off-limits to disagreement. The only supposedly legitimate persons allowed by the media to express any views whatsoever on Lebanon/Israel/Palestinians/U.S.-Middle-East policies were whitemen. Everyone else was either an Arab (i.e. "Anti-Semitic") or "Anti-Semitic," or else "self-hating Jews" (i.e. "Anti-Semitic").

With the construction of an ultimate taboo, a taboo behind which the fate of an entire people, the Palestinians, might be erased, how could there be an intellectual, a moral life after Lebanon in this country?

I would have to answer my own question in this way: Because many people in the United States and around the globe are not now nor have they ever been whitemen.

Many of these people are Black—one of whom tried to become President of our country. Many of these people are Jewish women who never quit from sending out flyers and making phone calls. Many of these people are male and female Jewish lawyers who are now personally threatened by new Reagan legislation intended to eliminate basic freedoms of dissent. Many of these people are young white women and young whitemen who do not want to grow up guilty of killing other people who have never hurt them. Many of these people are Black women and white women who perceive that the ambitions of self respect and species' survival reveal deeply indistinguishable values.

Here and in South Africa and in Nicaragua and in Amsterdam and in England I see a New Woman: She frequently wears a uniform. She often carries a gun. She puts down her body to block missiles and bullets, alike. She grieves for the dead but she fights back, to honor the dead. She learns self-defense. She runs for public office. She earns positions of enormous political power. And she is not calm. She is very excited and very busy making over this place into a safe place for us all, including whitemen.

She is Fannie Lou Hamer and Geraldine Ferrarro. She is Barbara Masakela and Winnie Mandela. She is Vivian Stromberg of Mobilization for Survival. She is Kathy Engel and Alexis De Veaux of MADRE. She is Carol Haddad who founded the Arab-American Women's Feminist League. She is Gail Jack-

son and Paula Finn of Art Against Apartheid. She is Sara Miles of
Talking Nicaragua and The International Brigades to Nicaragua.
She is Betsy Cohn who founded The Central American Historical
Institute in Washington. She is Frances Fox Piven who co-
founded The Human Serve Voter Registration movement that
may permanently alter the composition of our electorate.

She is Etel Adnan, the visionary, great Lebanese poet who
has written, in her transcendant, miraculous novel, *Sitt-Marie
Rose*:

> On the wall there is a crucifix. But, in this room, Christ is
> a tribal prince. He leads to nothing but ruin. One is never
> right to invoke him in such circumstances, because the
> true Christ only exists when one stands up to one's own
> brothers to defend the Stranger.

As a child I was taught that to tell the truth was often painful. As
an adult I have learned that not to tell the truth is more painful,
and that the fear of telling the truth—whatever the truth may
be—that fear is the most painful sensation of a moral life.

In my own life after Lebanon it has been other women who
have helped me to outlive and to undo my fears of telling the truth.
It is other women, the New Women among us, who have helped me
to see what the headlines and the powerful who seek to divide us
try to obscure and obliterate.

And I keep hearing about anti-Semitism. I read about Blacks
and Jews at "each other's throats." I am buffeted about by news of
phony freedom fighters and savage "victories" and "spheres of
influence" and "implacable" ethnic and ideological and class differences inevitably exploding to consume the earth. But what I see
for myself is New Women everywhere in the world discovering
each other with a happiness and a resolute purpose of survival
that will surpass all the weird and fatal bewitcheries of traditional
power, traditional insanities of conflict.

What I know from my own life after Lebanon is that I must
insist upon my own truth and my own love, especially when that
truth and that love will carry me across the borders of my own
tribe, or I will wither in the narrow cold light of my own eyes.

As Etel Adnan has written: It is when we women, The New
Women of the world, "Stand up to our brothers to defend the
Stranger," it is only then that we can hope to become innocent of
the evil that now imperils the planet. It is only then, when we cease

worshipping the tribe, that we will find our way into a tenable family of men and women as large and as invincible as infinite, infinitely varied, life.

Chapter 11

The Difficult Miracle of Black Poetry in America
or
Something Like a Sonnet for Phillis Wheatley
February, 1985

It was not natural. And she was the first. Come from a country of many tongues tortured by rupture, by theft, by travel like mismatched clothing packed down into the cargo hold of evil ships sailing, irreversible, into slavery. Come to a country to be docile and dumb, to be big and breeding, easily, to be turkey/horse/cow, to be cook/carpenter/plow, to be 5'6" 140 lbs., in good condition and answering to the name of Tom or Mary: to be bed bait: to be legally spread legs for rape by the master/the master's son/the master's overseer/the master's visiting nephew: to be nothing human nothing family nothing from nowhere nothing that-screams nothing that weeps nothing that dreams nothing that keeps anything/anyone deep in your heart: to live forcibly illiterate, forcibly itinerant: to live eyes lowered head bowed: to be worked without rest, to be worked without pay, to be worked without thanks, to be worked day up to nightfall: to be three-fifths of a human being at best: to be this valuable/this hated thing among strangers who purchased your life and then cursed it unceasingly: to be a slave: to be a slave. Come to this country a slave and how should you sing? After the flogging the lynch rope the general terror and weariness what should you know of a lyrical life? How could you, belonging to no one, but property to those despising the smiles of your soul, how could you dare to create yourself: a poet?

A poet can read. A poet can write.

A poet is African in Africa, or Irish in Ireland, or French on the left bank of Paris, or white in Wisconsin. A poet writes in her own language. A poet writes of her own people, her own history, her own vision, her own room, her own house where she sits at her own

87

table quietly placing one word after another word until she builds a line and a movement and an image and a meaning that somersaults all of these into the singing, the absolutely individual voice of the poet: at liberty. A poet is somebody free. A poet is someone at home.

How should there be Black poets in America?

It was not natural. And she was the first. It was 1761—so far back before the revolution that produced these United States, so far back before the concept of freedom disturbed the insolent crimes of this continent—in 1761, when seven year old Phillis stood, as she must, when she stood nearly naked, as small as a seven year old, by herself, standing on land at last, at last after the long, annihilating horrors of the Middle Passage. Phillis, standing on the auctioneer's rude platform: Phillis For Sale.

Was it a nice day?

Does it matter? Should she muse on the sky or remember the sea? Until then Phillis had been somebody's child. Now she was about to become somebody's slave.

Suzannah and John Wheatley finished their breakfast and ordered the carriage brought 'round. They would ride to the auction. This would be an important outing. They planned to buy yet another human being to help with the happiness of their comfortable life in Boston. You don't buy a human being, you don't purchase a slave, without thinking ahead. So they had planned this excursion. They were dressed for the occasion, and excited, probably. And experienced, certainly. The Wheatleys already owned several slaves. They had done this before; the transaction would not startle or confound or embarrass or appall either one of them.

Was it a nice day?

When the Wheatleys arrived at the auction they greeted their neighbors, they enjoyed this business of mingling with other townsfolk politely shifting about the platform, politely adjusting positions for gain of a better view of the bodies for sale. The Wheatleys were good people. They were kind people. They were openminded and thoughtful. They looked at the bodies for sale. They looked and they looked. This one could be useful for that. That one might be useful for this. But then they looked at that child, that Black child standing nearly naked, by herself. Seven or eight years old, at the most, and frail. Now that was a different proposal! Not a strong body, not a grown set of shoulders, not a promising wide set of hips, but a little body, a delicate body, a

young, surely terrified face! John Wheatley agreed to the whim of
his wife, Suzannah. He put in his bid. He put down his cash. He
called out the numbers. He competed successfully. He had a good
time. He got what he wanted. He purchased yet another slave. He
bought that Black girl standing on the platform, nearly naked. He
gave this new slave to his wife and Suzannah Wheatley was
delighted. She and her husband went home. They rode there by
carriage. They took that new slave with them. An old slave com-
manded the horses that pulled the carriage that carried the Wheatleys home, along with the new slave, that little girl they named
Phillis.

Why did they give her that name?

Was it a nice day?

Does it matter?

It was not natural. And she was the first: Phillis Miracle:
Phillis Miracle Wheatley: the first Black human being to be pub-
lished in America. She was the second female to be published in
America.

And the miracle begins in Africa. It was there that a bitterly
anonymous man and a woman conjoined to create this genius, this
lost child of such prodigious aptitude and such beguiling attributes that she very soon interposed the reality of her particular,
dear life between the Wheatleys' notions about slaves and the
predictable outcome of such usual blasphemies against Black
human beings.

Seven year old Phillis changed the slaveholding Wheatleys.
She altered their minds. She entered their hearts. She made them
see her and when they truly saw her, Phillis, darkly amazing them
with the sweetness of her spirit and the alacrity of her forbidden,
strange intelligence, they, in their own way, loved her as a prod-
igy, as a girl mysterious but godly.

Sixteen months after her entry into the Wheatley household
Phillis was talking the language of her owners. Phillis was flu-
ently reading the Scriptures. At eight and a half years of age, this
Black child, or "Africa's Muse," as she would later describe herself, was fully literate in the language of this slaveholding land.
She was competent and eagerly asking for more: more books, more
and more information. And Suzannah Wheatley loved this child of
her whimsical good luck. It pleased her to teach and to train and to
tutor this Black girl, this Black darling of God. And so Phillis
delved into kitchen studies commensurate, finally, to a classical
education available to young white men at Harvard.

She was nine years old.

What did she read? What did she memorize? What did the Wheatleys give to this African child? Of course, it was white, all of it: white. It was English, most of it, from England. It was written, all of it, by white men taking their pleasure, their walks, their pipes, their pens and their paper, rather seriously, while somebody else cleaned the house, washed the clothes, cooked the food, watched the children: probably not slaves, but possibly a servant, or, commonly, a wife. It was written, this white man's literature of England, while somebody else did the other things that have to be done. And that was the literature absorbed by the slave, Phillis Wheatley. That was the writing, the thoughts, the nostalgia, the lust, the conceits, the ambitions, the mannerisms, the games, the illusions, the discoveries, the filth and the flowers that filled up the mind of the African child.

At fourteen, Phillis published her first poem, "To the University of Cambridge": not a brief limerick or desultory teenager's verse, but thirty-two lines of blank verse telling those fellows what for and whereas, according to their own strict Christian codes of behavior. It is in that poem that Phillis describes the miracle of her own Black poetry in America:

While an intrinsic ardor bids me write
the muse doth promise to assist my pen

She says that her poetry results from "an intrinsic ardor," not to dismiss the extraordinary kindness of the Wheatleys, and not to diminish the wealth of white men's literature with which she found herself quite saturated, but it was none of these extrinsic factors that compelled the labors of her poetry. It was she who created herself a poet, notwithstanding and in despite of everything around her.

Two years later, Phillis Wheatley, at the age of sixteen, had composed three additional, noteworthy poems. This is one of them, "On Being Brought from Africa to America":

Twas mercy brought me from my Pagan land,
Taught my benighted soul to understand
That there's a God,that there's a Savior too:
Once I redemption neither sought nor knew
Some view our sable race with scornful eye,
"Their color is a diabolic die."
Remember, *Christians*, Negroes, black as Cain,
May be refin'd, and join the angelic train.

Where did Phillis get these ideas?

It's simple enough to track the nonsense about herself "benighted": *benighted* means surrounded and preyed upon by darkness. That clearly reverses what had happened to that African child, surrounded by and captured by the greed of white men. Nor should we find puzzling her depiction of Africa as "Pagan" versus somewhere "refined." Even her bizarre interpretation of slavery's theft of Black life as a merciful rescue should not bewilder anyone. These are regular kinds of iniquitous nonsense found in white literature, the literature that Phillis Wheatley assimilated, with no choice in the matter.

But here, in this surprising poem, this first Black poet presents us with something wholly her own, something entirely new. It is her matter of fact assertion that, "Once I redemption neither sought nor knew," as in: once I existed beyond and without these terms under consideration. *Once I existed on other than your terms.* And, she says, *but* since we are talking your talk about good and evil/redemption and damnation, let me tell you something you had better understand. I am Black as Cain *and* I may very well be an angel of the Lord. Take care not to offend the Lord!

Where did that thought come to Phillis Wheatley?

Was it a nice day?

Does it matter?

Following her "intrinsic ardor," and attuned to the core of her own person, this girl, the first Black poet in America, had dared to redefine herself from house slave to, possibly, an angel of the Almighty.

She was making herself at home.

And, depending whether you estimated that nearly naked Black girl on the auction block to be seven or eight years old, in 1761, by the time she was eighteen or nineteen, she had published her first book of poetry, *Poems on Various Subjects Religious and Moral.* It was published in London, in 1773, and the American edition appeared, years later, in 1786. Here are some examples from the poems of Phillis Wheatley:

From "On the Death of Rev. Dr. Sewell":

Come let us all behold with wishful eyes
The saint ascending to his native skies.

From "On the Death of the Rev. Mr. George Whitefield":

Take him, ye Africans, he longs for you,

Impartial Savior is his title due,
Washed in the fountain of redeeming blood,
You shall be sons and kings, and priest to God.

Here is an especially graceful and musical couplet, penned by the first Black poet in America:

But, see the softly stealing tears apace,
Pursue each other down the mourner's face;

This is an especially awful, virtually absurd set of lines by Ms. Wheatley:

"Go Thebons! great nations will obey
And pious tribute to her altars pay:
With rights divine, the goddess be implor'd,
Nor be her sacred offspring nor ador'd."
Thus Manto spoke. The Thebon maids obey,
And pious tribute to the goddess pay.

Awful, yes. Virtually absurd; well, yes, except, consider what it took for that young African to undertake such personal abstraction and mythologies a million million miles remote from her own ancestry, and her own darkly formulating face! Consider what might meet her laborings, as poet, should she, instead, invent a vernacular precise to Senegal, precise to slavery, and, therefore, accurate to the secret wishings of her lost and secret heart?

If she, this genius teenager, should, instead of writing verse to comfort a white man upon the death of his wife, or a white woman upon the death of her husband, or verse commemorating weirdly fabled white characters bereft of children diabolically dispersed; if she, instead composed a poetry to speak her pain, to say her grief, to find her parents, or to stir her people into insurrection, what would we now know about God's darling girl, that Phillis?

Who would publish that poetry, then?

But Phillis Miracle, she managed, nonetheless, to write, sometimes, towards the personal truth of her experience.

For example, we find in a monumental poem entitled "Thoughts on the Works of Providence," these five provocative lines, confirming every suspicion that most of the published Phillis Wheatley represents a meager portion of her concerns and inclinations:

As reason's pow'rs by day our God disclose,
So we may trace him in the night's repose.
Say what is sleep? and dreams how passing strange!

When action ceases, and ideas range
Licentious and unbounded o'er the plains.

And, concluding this long work, there are these lines:

Infinite *love* whene'er we turn our eyes
Appears: this ev'ry creature's wants supplies,
This most is heard in Nature's constant voice,
This makes the morn, and this the eve rejoice,
This bids the fost'ring rains and dews descend
To nourish all, to serve one gen'ral end,
The good of man: Yet man ungrateful pays
But little homage, and but little praise.

Now and again and again these surviving works of the genius
Phillis Wheatley veer incisive and unmistakable, completely
away from the verse of good girl Phillis ever compassionate upon
the death of someone else's beloved, pious Phillis modestly enrap-
tured by the glorious trials of virtue on the road to Christ, arcane
Phillis intent upon an "Ode to Neptune," or patriotic Phillis pen-
ning an encomium to General George Washington ("Thee, first in
peace and honor"). Then do we find that "Ethiop,' as she once
called herself, that "Africa's muse," knowledgeable but succinct,
on "dreams how passing strange!/When action ceases, and ideas
range/Licentious and unbounded o'er the plains."

Phillis Licentious Wheatley?

Phillis Miracle Wheatley in contemplation of love and want of
love?

Was it a nice day?

It was not natural. And she was the first.

Repeatedly singing for liberty, singing against the tyrannical, repeatedly avid in her trusting support of the American Revolution (how could men want freedom enough to die for it but then
want slavery enough to die for that?) repeatedly lifting witness to
the righteous and the kindly factors of her days, this was no
ordinary teenaged poet, male or female, Black or white. Indeed, the
insistently concrete content of her tribute to the revolutionaries
who would forge America, an independent nation state, indeed the
specific daily substance of her poetry establishes Phillis Wheatley
as the first decidedly American poet on this continent, Black or
white, male or female.

Nor did she only love the ones who purchased her, a slave,
those ones who loved her, yes, but with astonishment. Her lifelong
friend was a young Black woman, Obour Tanner, who lived in

Newport, Rhode Island, and one of her few poems dedicated to a living person, neither morbid nor ethereal, was written to the young Black visual artist Sapio Moorhead, himself a slave. It is he who crafted the portrait of Phillis that serves as her frontispiece profile in her book of poems. Here are the opening lines from her poem, "To S.M., A Young African Painter, On Seeing His Works."

> To show the lab'ring bosom's deep intent,
> And thought in living characters to paint.
> When first thy pencil did those beauties give,
> And breathing figures learnt from thee to live,
> How did those prospects give my soul delight,
> A new creation rushing on my sight?
> Still, wondrous youth! each noble path pursue,
> On deathless glories fix thine ardent view:
> Still may the painter's and the poet's fire
> To aid thy pencil, and thy verse conspire!
> And many the charms of each seraphic theme
> Conduct thy footsteps to immortal fame!

Remember that the poet so generously addressing the "wondrous youth" is certainly no older than eighteen, herself! And this, years before the American Revolution, and how many many years before the 1960s! This is the first Black poet of America addressing her Brother Artist not as so-and-so's Boy, but as "Scipio Moorhead, A Youg African Painter."

Where did Phillis Miracle acquire this consciousness?

Was it a nice day?

It was not natural. And she was the first.

But did she—we may persevere, critical from the ease of the 1980s—did she love, did she need, freedom?

In the poem (typically titled at such length and in such deferential rectitude as to discourage most readers from scanning what follows), in the poem titled "To the Right Honorable William, Earl of Dartmouth, His Majesty's Principal Secretary of State for North America, etc.," Phillis Miracle has written these irresistible, authentic, felt lines:

> No more America in mournful strain
> Of wrongs, and grievance unredress'd complain,
> No longer shalt Thou dread the iron chain,
> Which wanton tyranny with lawless head
> Had made, and with it meant t' enslave the land.
> Should you, my Lord, while you peruse my song,

Wonder from whence my love of Freedom sprung,
Whence flow these wishes for the common good,
By feeling hearts alone best understood,
I, young in life, by seeming cruel of fate
Was snatch'd from Afric's fancy'd happy seat.
What pangs excruciating must molest
What sorrows labour in my parent's breast?
Steel'd was that soul and by no misery mov'd
That from a father seized his babe belov'd
Such, such my case. And can I then but pray
Others may never feel tyrannic sway?

So did the darling girl of God compose her thoughts, prior to 1772.

And then.

And then her poetry, these poems, were published in London.

And then, during her twenty-first year, Suzannah Wheatley, the white woman slaveholder who had been changed into the white mother, the white mentor, the white protector of Phillis, died.

Without that white indulgence, that white love, without that white sponsorship, what happened to the young African daughter, the young African poet?

No one knows for sure.

With the death of Mrs. Wheatley, Phillis came of age, a Black slave in America.

Where did she live?

How did she eat?

No one knows for sure.

But four years later she met and married a Black man, John Peters. Mr. Peters apparently thought well of himself, and of his people. He comported himself with dignity, studied law, argued for the liberation of Black people, and earned the everyday dislike of white folks. His wife bore him three children; all of them died.

His wife continued to be Phillis Miracle.

His wife continued to obey the "intrinsic ardor" of her calling and she never ceased the practice of her poetry. She hoped, in fact, to publish a second volume of her verse.

This would be the poetry of Phillis the lover of John, Phillis the woman, Phillis the wife of a Black man pragmatically premature in his defiant self-respect, Phillis giving birth to three children, Phillis, the mother, who must bury the three children she delivered into American life.

None of these poems was ever published.

This would have been the poetry of someone who had chosen herself, free, and brave to be free in a land of slavery.

When she was thirty-one years old, in 1784, Phillis Wheatley, the first Black poet in America, she died.

Her husband, John Peters, advertised and begged that the manuscript of her poems she had given to someone, please be returned. But no one returned them.

*And I believe we would not have seen them, anyway. I believe no one would have published the poetry of Black Phillis Wheatley, that grown woman who stayed with her chosen Black man. I believe that the death of Suzannah Wheatley, coincident with the African poet's twenty-first birthday, signalled, decisively, the end of her status as a child, as a dependent. From there we would hear from an independent Black woman poet in America.

Can you imagine that, in 1775?

Can you imagine that, today?

America has long been tolerant of Black children, compared to its reception of independent Black men and Black women.

She died in 1784.

Was it a nice day?

It was not natural. And she was the first.

Last week, as the final judge for this year's Loft McKnight Awards in creative writing, awards distributed in Minneapolis, Minnesota, I read through sixteen manuscripts of rather fine poetry.

These are the terms, the lexical items, that I encountered there:

Rock, moon, star, roses, chimney, Prague, elms, lilac, railroad tracks, lake, lilies, snow geese, crow, mountain, arrow feathers, ear of corn, marsh, sandstone, rabbit-bush, gulley, pumpkins, eagle, tundra, dwarf willow, dipper-bird, brown creek, lizards, sycamores, glacier, canteen, skate eggs, birch, spruce, pumphandle

Is anything about that listing odd? I didn't suppose so. These are the terms, the lexical items accurate to the specific white Minnesota daily life of those white poets.

And so I did not reject these poems, I did not despise them saying, "How is this possible? Sixteen different manuscripts of poetry written in 1985 and not one of them uses the terms of my own Black life! Not one of them writes about the police murder of

Eleanor Bumpurs or the Bernard Goetz shooting of four Black boys or apartheid in South Africa, or unemployment, or famine in Ethiopia, or rape, or fire escapes, or cruise missiles in the New York harbor, or medicare, or alleyways, or napalm, or $4.00 an hour, and no time off for lunch.

I did not and I would not presume to impose my urgencies upon white poets writing in America. But the miracle of Black poetry in America, the *difficult* miracle of Black poetry in America, is that we have been rejected and we are frequently dismissed as "political" or "topical" or "sloganeering" and "crude" and "insignificant" because, like Phillis Wheatley, we have persisted for freedom. We will write against South Africa and we will seldom pen a poem about wild geese flying over Prague, or grizzlies at the rain barrel under the dwarf willow trees. We will write, published or not, however we may, like Phillis Wheatley, of the terror and the hungering and the quandaries of our African lives on this North American soil. And as long as we study white literature, as long as we assimilate the English language and its implicit English values, as long as we allude and defer to gods we "neither sought nor knew," as long as we, Black poets in America, remain the children of slavery, as long as we do not come of age and attempt, then to speak the truth of our difficult maturity in an alien place, alien place, then we will be beloved, and sheltered, and published,

But not otherwise. And yet we persist.

And it was not natural. And she was the first.

This is the difficult miracle of Black poetry in America: that we persist, published or not, and loved or unloved: we persist.

And this is: "Something Like A Sonnet for Phillis Miracle Wheatley":

Girl from the realm of birds florid and fleet
flying full feather in far or near weather
Who fell to a dollar lust coffled like meat
Captured by avarice and hate spit together
Trembling asthmatic alone on the slave block
built by a savagery travelling by carriage
viewed like a species of flaw in the livestock
A child without safety of mother or marriage

Chosen by whimsy but born to surprise
They taught you to read but you learned how to write
Begging the universe into your eyes:

They dressed you in light but you dreamed
with the night.
From Africa singing of justice and grace,
Your early verse sweetens the fame of our Race.

And because we Black people in North America persist in an
irony profound, Black poetry persists in this way:

Like the trees of winter and
like the snow which has no power
makes very little sound
but comes and collects itself
edible light on the black trees
The tall black trees of winter
lifting up a poetry of snow
so that we may be astounded
by the poems of Black
trees inside a cold environment

Chapter 12

Black People and the Law:
A Tribute to William Kunstler
March, 1985

Back in the 1960s, a national movement of Black people sought to overthrow traditional guarantees of our contemptible status here in America. Repeatedly, we marched and we sang and we kneeled and we prayed and we sat down at coffee shop counters and we rode Greyhound buses and we attempted to use public bathrooms or we tried to stop our thirst by drinking a little cold water from public water fountains. And we did all of this at the risk of our multitudinous Black lives because we believed, absolutely, we believed in something almost holy.

We did not believe we could change the hearts of those who hated us. We did not believe that we could alter the ideological bent of those ever devising new systems for the degradation of the weak and the poor. But we believed that our fierce and our massive and our non-violent rebellions against racist tyranny would lead to a changing of the laws of this country. We believed in the law. We believed that a city ordinance or that State and Federal legislation could transform the habits and the potentiality of this multi-racial society so that minority groups need never tremble, again, at the evil meanings of *majority rule,* or *might makes right,* or *rule by force.*

Redemption from this North American purgatory of institutionalized and hallowed racism could not come to Black people through money—we did not have any of that; or through numbers—we were the few among the many who despised us; or through political power—we possessed no legal access to political power.

Our route to redemption was the law. If it is against the law to kill somebody, we reasoned, then, in a democratic nation state

99

founded on the precept that all men are created equal, it must follow that it is against the law for anybody to kill anybody else. Murder must be equally against the law, no matter if the killer is a white man, and the victim is a Black man, or a Black woman, or a Black boy.

But more than this, we reasoned that our civilization, from as long ago as Moses, when the Lord Almighty handed down the Tablets, and continuing up to the U.S. Supreme Court Decision of 1954, we reasoned that the law deserves to govern our conduct only insofar as it proves itself impartial, only insofar as it proves itself impervious to perversion by privilege.

We believed this. And in our faith we were fundamentalists. No one has ever believed in the law, in the power of the law to create and preserve justice among all people, more than the Black people of these United States. No one has ever trusted the founding words of the founding legal documents that defined this republic independent of England more than the Black people of these United States. From the whipmarks on our backs to the burial grounds for our dead, we knew the awesome power of the laws that decreed that a man who is a slave shall not escape his slavery. We knew the consequences of the law that decreed we should not read nor write nor marry nor vote nor raise our own children. What miraculous and profound change could we not accomplish, if only we could change the law!

And the laws did change. And one man, a white man, William Moses Kunstler, chose to enter our national history without fear and with much righteous and eloquent wrath. He earned his outstanding presence in our national consciousness through his own aggressive belief in the legal possibilities for justice: equality under the law.

A Phi Beta Kappa graduate from Yale, a graduate from Columbia Law School, William Kunstler could have chosen many other ways to expend his brilliant energies. But in the 1960s he chose to stand there, beside us. He chose to stay there, among us: the weak and the poor. Taking on Freedom Rider cases and school desegregation cases, and serving as Special Trial Counsel for Dr. Martin Luther King, Jr., this man, this Moses of our time, he fought and he fought to deliver the law from the disgrace of its perversions by privilege.

He fought and he won. Indeed, we fought and we won. By the end of the 1960s, as Black Americans, we had won huge and unarguable gains of liberty; we could vote, we could go to the bathroom, and we could go out and drink a cup of coffee, after all of that.

Legally entitled to every right of every citizen in the U.S.A., we arrived at the 1970s. Then came 1971. This is when I met Big Bill Kunstler for the first time. I was teaching at Yale, his alma mater. I had founded the Yale Attica Defense, along with several students. We had felt the absolute necessity of responding to the murder that came down because Governor Nelson Rockefeller ordered police, state troopers and prison guards—carrying big game .270 rifles and Ithaca Model 37 shotguns with double-buckshot—to post themselves on the overlooking rim of the D-yard, at Attica. They opened fire upon 1500 men penned below them: 1500 men and not one with a gun. The state murdered forty-three men: and not one of them with a gun.

Attica attested to the separating of the state from the law. Murder is against the law. Attica inaugurated an era of progressive lawlessness perpetuated by the powerful. From Rockefeller, in 1971, to Ronald Reagan's reference to the 1981 Boland Amendment as a mere "proposal," (the Boland Amendment is a Congressional law explicitly prohibiting United States' aggression against Nicaragua), from Rockefeller in 1971 to the Reagan administration's contempt for and withdrawal from the World Court; from Governor Rockefeller, in 1971, to the 1985 Grand Jury's attempted exoneration of the homicidal maniac, Bernard Goetz, we have travelled a conceivably irreversible, sinister road into the crisis now threatening the survival of nineteen year old Darrell Cabey, and Nicaragua, and First World peoples, generally, and all of our own selves, multi-racial citizens that we are, in North America.

It is the crisis of the state separating itself from the law. It is the crisis of the law overpowered by the power of the state. It is the crisis of the people of the state versus the power of the state that will not honor and fulfill the law except when it protects the powerful at the expense of the weak and the poor.

I remember that sunny morning in New Haven when I first met Big Bill Kunstler. He was running up the ceremonious wide stairs of a hall where an enormous crowd of students waited to ask him about the Attica Brothers. His glasses pushed up on his forehead, his overcoat lightly thrown around his broad shoulders, he looked like a mountain of a man coming towards me. And when he spoke, when I heard that extraordinarily deep voice filling up that splendid stairwell, I felt no longer exhausted by the phone calls, the flyers, and the rest of it. I felt exhilarlation and relief: I knew he would surely kick ass. And he did.

And he has been my steady friend since then. He has never failed me. From Attica to the episode years later when an article I was writing placed my life under threat, to last semester when twenty-five year old Reggie Jordan, the brother of one of my students, was shot eight times by police—four times in the back— Bill has been there for me: available by phone and otherwise.

He does not quit.

As he fought for the passage of Civil Rights laws, Bill Kunstler now fights for their enforcement. Although he has many times witnessed this nation violate the very civil rights it is supposed to protect, he remains a towering resource for justice, a towering warrior for the moral validity of this civilization— because he knows there is no other recourse for the weak and the poor. There is the law or there is nothing that will protect them against the trivial or the heinous misuse of power, by the powerful. And this is true everywhere in the world.

I thank him for the bravery and the virtue of his leadership.

In Our Hands
May, 1985

I remember when I first saw a washing machine: not a drawing or a photograph, but the machine itself. I must have been seven or eight years old. My mother announced that we were about to walk up Hancock Street together. "Where are we going?" I asked her. "To the corner," was her mysterious and complete reply.

On the corner there was something new. A Black man, a World War II veteran named Mr. Epps, had opened a very large Laundromat that was filled, my mother told me, with machines that could wash your clothes for you. I eagerly accompanied my mother on that walk. Unable to see anything definite through the store windows, we finally went inside. Mr. Epps stood near the door, ready to smile, introduce himself and gain a customer. He talked us over to one of the machines lined against the wall, dropped a nickel into the slot and let us watch, silently, as soapy water began to rise behind the glass. All the way through Mr. Epps's explanations, my mother said absolutely nothing. When he had finished talking, my mother simply thanked him and somberly declared that she would "think it over."

More than a month was to pass before my mother decided to "risk" any of our laundry to Mr. Epps and his machines. I pestered and prodded my mother: What was the "risk"? What could there be to "think over"? Sissey's mother used the machines. Carlyle's mother used them. If we couldn't be the first, did we have to be the last family on the block to use the Laundromat? It would be many years later before I could even guess at the reasons for her hesitation. The machines seemed too easy. That Laundromat could mean three or four hours less work for my mother ever week. But it would also mitigate her own familiar sense of virtue: the burden of her womanly toil.

I did see what washing the laundry demanded of her. It would usually be a Saturday morning. After cooking and serving me and my father breakfast, my mother would clear the table, wash up the dishes and the pots, dry these and put them away to make room for the ordeal of the laundry. Next she would strip the beds of the sheets, strip the bathroom of the towels, gather the dirty clothes and then fill the two kitchen sinks with water. Soap went into one of them, the one with the scrub board that made a fabulous drumming sound. After the clothes were rinsed, I would help my mother to drag the dripping sheets, piece by piece, out into the yard or down into the basement where we, together, twisted and twisted the heavy wet cotton until it was ready to go on the clothesline. Sometimes my mother borrowed a wringer that fit awkwardly on the edge of the sink and I would take a regular turn at it, squeezing the towels through and then shaking them free of wrinkles before hanging them up to dry.

I am talking about hard work: "woman's work." My mother didn't talk much, but she worked, everlastingly. Abandoned as an infant by her own mother, she had managed to grow up and, eventually, to get through high school by working her way into the good graces of the woman, the substitute mother, with whom she lived in a little mountain town in Jamaica. From the days of her early girlhood, my mother performed the random household functions of a servant, really, in order to secure food and shelter. When she reached the end of her teens, my mother had saved enough money to come to America; and so she came to New Jersey, to find her "real" mother and to see about becoming a nurse.

No one had ever suggested to her, no one had ever shown my mother, a kind of "woman's work" that might be easy or enjoyable or generally regarded as "important" or prestigious or recognizable as the invention of power. My mother had never heard of women who command militia units or chair international committees for human rights or piece together movements for the liberation of a people. What she knew was that, even as a child, she must devise a means of survival where nothing like that was readily available to her. What she knew was that surviving as a Black woman meant living on her own, depending absolutely on no one other than herself. (How many times did she warn me: No matter if you get married, you must know how to take care of yourself and the children, by yourself.) What she knew was that surviving as a Black woman meant hard, endless work that left her dark hands swollen and gray from the bleach in the laundry water and cracked from the ceaseless rubbing of the clothes against the rippled surface of the scrub board.

I think that she may even have verified the virtue of her life according to the weariness she felt at the close of a day. If she did not feel exhausted, there must be something still not done that she must do.

And as a child I noticed the sadness of my mother as she sat alone in the kitchen at night, eating dry crackers or drinking a cup of tea. Her woman's work never won permanent victories of any kind. It never enlarged the universe of her imagination or her power to influence what happened beyond the front door of our house. Her woman's work never tickled her to laugh or shout or dance.

But she did raise me to respect her way of offering love and to believe that hard work is often the irreducible factor for survival, not something to avoid. Her woman's work produced a reliable home base where I could pursue the privileges of books and music. Her woman's work invented the potential for a completely different kind of work for us, the next generation of Black women: huge, rewarding hard work demanded by the huge, new ambitions that her perfect confidence in us engendered.

Just yesterday I stood for a few minutes at the top of the stairs leading to a white doctor's office in a white neighborhood. I watched one Black woman after another trudge to the corner, where she then waited to catch the bus home. These were Black women still cleaning somebody else's house or Black women still caring for somebody else's sick or elderly, before they came back to the frequently thankless chores of their own loneliness, their own families. And I felt angry and I felt ashamed. And I felt, once again, the kindling heat of my hope that we, the daughters of these Black women, will honor their sacrifice by giving them thanks. We will undertake, with pride, every transcendent dream of freedom made possible by the humility of their love.

Chapter 14

The Blood Shall Be a Sign Unto You:[1]
Israel and South Africa

April, 1985

INTRODUCTION

I was invited to participate in The Foreign Policy Panel of the Socialist Scholars Conference, April 6, 1985, in New York City. The panel was organized by South End Press and it included the speakers Holly Sklar, Bogdan Denitch and Noam Chomsky. More than a month prior to the Conference I asked an editor at South End Press what the others would talk about. When I learned that no one else intended to address South Africa, I immediately decided to do this, myself. Because the Conference took place on the second day of Passover, which was also the day before Easter, I seized the occasion as a chance to appeal to progressive North American Blacks and Jews, for the creation of new solidarity centered on a very serious problem: the relationship between Israel and South Africa.

Given the explosively taboo status of the subject of Israel, I have quoted from other sources to an extensive, even extreme, degree. I am rather weary of all the bully efforts to isolate and discredit my own fact finding and analyses.

I wish to thank Benjamin Beit-Hallahmi, an editor of the Israeli monthly, New Outlook, *and Professor of Psychology at The University of Haifa, for our personal, and lengthy conversation subsequent to my presentation of this essay. We do not always agree, of course. Agreement is not the point. Mutual respect that can accommodate genuine disagreement is the civilized point of intellectual exchange, particularly in a political context. In any event, Beit-Hallahmi has devoted nine years to the preparation of his forthcoming book on Israel and the Third World. I certainly look forward to its publication, in English.*

As a child I learned the stories and the teachings of the Bible. Not some of them, not sections of the Scripture, but all of it—the Old and the New Testament—inundated my consciousness, daily. Sundays simply concluded another week of intense religious study and instruction.

I did not then suppose any great difference between the Hebrews who followed Moses out of Egypt and the Jews who followed Jesus into the Kingdom of Heaven. As I moved from Genesis through the Gospel according to Matthew, Luke, and John, I assumed I was moving across the history of one people, a people capable of incredible faith and incredible wrath, a people capable of producing Jesus, the Jewish Messiah, and a people capable of demanding his death, his crucifixion: A people, in short, like any other, encompassing the complete variety of regular human attributes, from evil to good. This did not surprise or confuse me.

I lived in a Negro ghetto, as a child. Everyone around me was nice or not nice or reliable or a liar or cruel or self sacrificing or abominable or fabulous but everyone, and I mean everybody, was Black. When I closed the Bible for the day, when I left the Israelites crossing the suddenly parted waters of the Red Sea, and when I turned to the actual house and the strict life of my own people, I found, among my own, a complexity of character and deed fully comparable to Cain and Abel, to Joseph and his brothers, to Jesus, Judas, and the Pharisees.

I did not then suppose any great difference between the Jews and my own people. Especially as a child I would admit no such concept as "a chosen people" unless I thought that concept included me. And, besides, beyond the commandments, for example, "thou shalt not kill" and "love thy neighbor as thyself," (commandments that seemed eminently sensible, and challenging, to my rather hot-tempered eight year old mind), there was this predicament that the long ago Hebrew tribes appeared to have shared with my people. It was the predicament of a persecuted minority. It was the dilemma of a people stolen into homelessness and forced into bondage. It was the quandary of the slave who will not believe "the mastery" of the master, let alone worship him.

When Moses said, "Let my people go," was that not an obvious thing to say? Is there any other response to the imposition of one people's wishes and ways upon another? With all of my needs and with all of my desires, how could I not understand those four words as a Black girl living here? *Let my people go.*

And, as for a difference between Passover and Easter, or between one righteous escape from death and another righteous escape from death, I did not see it. I did not see any difference.

Now it is 1985. And I am no longer a child. I know that neither my people, here in North America, nor the Jews of North America, nor the Jews of Israel, live under the worst form of persecution, confront the worst threats to our security as distinctive peoples, possess the smallest capacities for self-defense, or work against the greatest hungers of the world.

Compared to anybody in Nicaragua, I am fat, I am safe, and I am rich. Compared to any Palestinian refugee, the Jews of Israel are fat, safe, and rich.

In momentously different ways, and to importantly different depths, Blacks and Jews have, nonetheless, set ourselves free from most extremities of aggression against us. Our problems are no longer the same problems. For one thing, the distribution of power is very different between us. And I am pursuing these ideas only because I believe that we, progressive Blacks and Jews of North America, can, together, control and rightly alter the meaning of that difference of power.

It is 1985. And there is Israel. And there is South Africa. That is the standing difference between us: Blacks and Jews of North America. For anyone Jewish, I would imagine that Israel must represent, on a level of sensibility inaccessible to argument and/or entreaty, an absolute imperative, a refuge, a place of sanctuary, a final deliverance out of the deserts of horror.

This is nothing to discuss or dispute. This is Israel.

Anyone certifiably Jewish is welcome to emigrate to Israel. Inside Israel, anyone certifiably Jewish can vote, can appear as a fully entitled citizen in a court of law. Inside Israel, anyone certifiably Jewish can choose where he or she will settle, can move freely about the entire nation, can travel outside the country and then return. Inside Israel, anyone certifiably Jewish enjoys civil liberties pertinent to education, freedom of speech, rights of assembly, democratic representation, and the right to bear arms. Inside Israel, anyone certifiably Jewish is protected by the State from State intrusion upon his or her privacy of thought and dwelling space. Inside Israel, the absolute ruling majority of the people is Jewish. Inside Israel, no one not certifiably Jewish may assume these same rights, or accede to the same benefits of citizenship.

But is Israel safe?

With a total population of roughly more than four million, Israel is, today, the fourth largest military power in the world.[2]

But is Israel isolated and without powerful allies?

In his *Fateful Triangle*, a monumental and fastidiously documented work, Noam Chomsky reports: "For fiscal years 1978 through 1982, Israel received 48% of all U.S. economic aid, worldwide."[3] Since 1982, U.S. aid to Israel has not diminished; it has increased. This extraordinary commitment to the support of Israel clearly describes its unquestioned, favored ranking in the eyes of one of Israel's two most powerful allies, namely, the United States. The other powerful Israeli ally is South Africa.

The Israeli writer, Benjamin Beit-Hallahmi, itemizes a number of the special facts peculiar to the Israeli-South African alliance:

> *The Lavi jet, another major Israeli achievement is also an Israeli-South African joint production. *The two air forces have been training together for at least ten years, as have the two navies.*[4]
>
> *The joint Israeli-South African nuclear program has been reported on by sources in both countries. Israel has also supplied South Africa with Jericho missiles, capable of carrying a nuclear warhead.[5]
>
> *Israel is the only foreign country to have considerable investments in the four Bantustan states created by South Africa.[6]
>
> *Yitzhak Rabin, currently Israel's defense minister, said in April 1976, when he was prime minister, that South Africa and Israel shared the same ideals.[7]

In *Israeli Foreign Affairs* March 1985, I have found this information:

> In 1974, after the UN condemned the 'unholy alliance' between the two nations, and after all but four Black African nations broke relations with Israel, Yossel Lapid, chief of Israeli Radio and Televsion, said, 'If we have to choose between friendship, with Black Africa, as it is today, and friendship with a white, well-organized and successful country with a booming Jewish community, then I prefer South Africa.'[8]

In the London *Sunday Times*, April 15, 1985, James Adams, author of *The Unnatural Alliance*, and defense correspondent of the *Sunday Times* has written, "According to the International Monetary Fund, South African trade with Israel is minute, representing only 0.6% of the former's total exports and only 0.5% of its imports, very little compared, for instance, with South Africa's trade with the United States. However, official figures take no account of the trade in diamonds or military equipment. Military sales are considered too sensitive to be discussed publicly, while all diamond sales by South Africa to any country are confidential."

Furthermore, Adams reports:

Israel has shared much of its nuclear technology with South Africa. As early as 1968, Professor Ernst Bergmann, the father of Israel's nuclear programme, told an audience at the South African Institute of International Affairs at Jan Smith's House in Johannesburg: "In general I have found that, in nuclear physics, the two countries are verging on not only similar, but almost identical, lines. I have discussed with my colleagues— whether collaboration between the two countries might not be of some value. I was glad to find a very enthusiastic response. I think we can formulate the common problem in the similarity of our two countries by saying, 'Neither of us has neighbors to whom we can speak and to whom we are going to be able to speak in the near future. If we are in this position of isolation, perhaps it might be best for both countries to speak to each other.'"[9]

Adams follows Bergmann's remarks with this comment: "The nuclear relationship has progressed considerably since Bergmann's day on a basis of exchanging uranium from South Africa for technology from Israel."[10]

It is the prospering development of such an exchange—South African raw materials and "cheap labor," for Israeli technology— that enlivens the prospect of these two white powers becoming absolutely self-sufficient, as regards the world beyond their collaboration. One of them may, then, successfully dominate Southern Africa and the other of them the North.

As reported by the *New York Times*, August 5, 1984, the South African Foreign Minister, Roelof F. Botha, "met today with Yitzhak Shamir, his Israeli counterpart, as part of what Israeli officers described as a "private visit." *The New York Times* article continues, "The visit by the South African Foreign Minister appeared to be causing some minor embarassment to Israeli officials. Although Mr. Botha's visit is being described as private, he was met at the airport Sunday night by Mr. Shamir and provided with an official limousine and all the usual courtesies of an official visit, including a dinner this evening."

Taking this alliance, "unholy"[11] or otherwise, to yet another level, Roy Iscowitz has reported, in *The Jerusalem Post*,

> It is easy to dismiss last week's 'Twin Cities' agreement between the West Bank Settlement of Ariel and Bishop, capital of the South African homeland, Cisker, as dismal and grotesque..The Israeli speakers, among whom were Likud Knesset member Yoram Aridor, Haim Kaufman and Michael Dekel, spoke in terms of Israeli-Ciskeran brotherhood and a common struggle against a cruel world of double standards...In the three years since he accepted 'independence' from South Africa, (Ciskeran) President-for-life Sebe has imposed a reign of terror on his people that has left even his apartheid mentors aghast.[12]

Unfortunately, these actions by Israelis, and this alliance between Israel and South Africa, do not extrude themselves as egregious and peculiar and exceptional to an otherwise humane and readily defensible pattern of chosen international Israeli functions.

> Consider any third world area that has been a trouble spot in the past ten years and you will discover Israeli officers and weapons implicated in the conflict supporting America's interests and helping in what they call 'the defense of the West.' The symbols of this involvement are as familiar as the Uzi submachine gun and the Galil assault rifle, and Israeli officers named Lzi and Galil and Golen. They can be found in Iran, Nicaragua, El Salvador, Guatemala, Haiti, Namibia, Taiwan, Indonesia, The Philippines, Chile and Bolivia...to name a few ...There is virtually no Israeli opposition to this global adventurism. There is no 'human rights' lobby to oppose military involvement in Guatemala, Haiti, or South Africa.[13]

As a child, my whole being reverberated to the four words, *Let my people go*. And I thought that these words emphatically spoke to the needs of my people, Black people in America, and to the Jewish people, the Israelites of the Bible, and of our time.

I am no longer a child. I know that neither my people's needs nor the needs of the Jewish people any longer compare to the enormous desperate needs of the Palestinians and the peoples of Nicaragua, El Salvador, Guatemala, the Philippines, Chile, and Namibia. I know that it would be an obscenity for me, or for my people here in North America, to propose any serious comparison between the continuing, grave difficulties of our unwanted residency here in America with the almost unspeakable, the exhaustive, the boastful and annihilating evils of apartheid.

And how should the Israelis compare themselves to the Black Africans who struggle and who perish under apartheid?

There is Israel. There is South Africa. That is the ultimate standing difference between Blacks and Jews, in North America.

For everyone Black in this country, I know I may speak on this subject, as I may speak for myself: South Africa represents racist doom, racist purgatory, and racist violence almost byzantine in the precision and the thoroughness of its conception and its relentless application. South Africa is all of the feelings and all of the social implications of the world's hatred of Black people brought to an absolutely heinous—brought to an almost almighty— fruition. South Africa is our holocaust.

South Africa is not the Egyptian bondage of the Israelites. South Africa is not the American enslavement of Africans. South Africa is not the Nazi extermination of the Jews. South Africa is not the American segregation of Afro-Americans into second and third class citizenship. South Africa is right now, today, proceeding to murder, to dispossess, to debase, to break apart, to forcibly resettle and to legislate into peonage the Black African peoples to whom that land rightfully belongs.

In South Africa, Africans numbered 22.7 million as against 4.7 million whites. In South Africa, Africans cannot vote. Constituting more that 72% of the total population inside South Africa, Africans must live on 13% of the land, the poorest, least arable land, or they must join the 3.5 million Africans whom the Afrikaners have forcibly "resettled" into the hideous, barren Bantustans, since 1960. Inside South Africa, Africans possess no freedom of movement within the country. Inside South Africa, except for one or two weeks every year, African men must live apart from their wives and children, or they must forfeit the miserable employment relegated to them by whites. In 1982, inside South Africa, "the average monthly wage was $1136 for whites and $250 for Africans. For every $1.00 that a white employee earns, an African earns 22 cents. In 1982, inside South Africa, "the government spent $1199 on education for every white child and $145 for every African child."

Inside South Africa, Africans have no legal rights whatsoever. They do not have freedom of speech, freedom of assembly or the right to bear arms. In South Africa, Africans have nothing but holocaust, a situation of great destruction erected against their literal existence as human beings. South Africa is an everyday holocaust. How is it possible that Israel should trade with South Africa? How is it possible that Israel should collaborate with South Africa? How is it possible that Israel should welcome the foreign minister in Israel? How is it possible that Israel should celebrate the Twin City arrangement between the West Bank settlement of Ariel and the despotic bantustan of Cisker? What does this mean? I believe this means that the Jews of the world are one people like any other: neither morally superior nor more evil than any other. I believe that suffering does not confer virtue upon the victim. Hence it is possible that the slave will become the slaveholder and that the victim will become the executioner.

President-for-life Lenox Sebe is African-born and raised inside South Africa. It is his African despotism that now imperils the lives of his unwilling citizenry: all of them forced African refugees from South Africa. I believe that neither good nor evil is an inherent attribute of any people or any human being. Hence we have African despots and despotic African regimes elsewhere on the continent of Africa. After the bloody revolutions required for independence from white colonial tyrants, these Africans now emulate those tyrants in their corrupt African administrations: they impose inequities and they violently suppress dissent. Hence, after the many thousands of years history of the Jews as the hated stranger on the planet, as the weak minority everywhere persecuted by those more powerful than they, we have Israel allied with South Africa, Israel dispossessing and decimating the Palestinians, Israel supporting Somoza and every other tyrannical regime in the Third and First Worlds upon request. *Morality is an existential undertaking.* It is something each of us must evaluate moment by moment. I may have been dominated and oppressed by people different from me and stronger than I am but surely I may dominate and oppress people different from me and weaker than I am. No matter how powerless I may be there is always someone more powerless than I. That weaker human being may become my victim at any minute. It is obvious to me that I have acted the tyrant toward and actively dominated those who are, for instance, younger and smaller than I am. Not always, I hope. But sometimes, yes.

I know I may speak for my people, the Black people of North America as I may speak for myself when I tell you that I am prepared to give my life for the righteous liberation of the Africans of South Africa. I will not cease in my struggles to support that coming victory until all of us may celebrate the accomplishment of African majority rule in South Africa. This means that every ally of apartheid, every policy supporting apartheid is my enemy. This means that I must call upon all progressive Blacks and Jews of North America to oppose the "constructive engagement" of the Reagan administration with South Africa in each of its covert and overt respects. This means that I must call upon all the progressive Blacks and Jews of North America to condemn the Israeli alliance with South Africa in each of its covert and overt respects. We must effectively mount political and economic sanctions against every U.S. official and every U.S. corporation that in any way collaborates with South Africa. We must effectively mount political and economic sanctions against any country, any politician, any corporation, British/French/ Israeli that in any way collaborates with South Africa.

Among developed countries the United States is clearly the most powerful and the most resourceful ally of counterrevolutionary, inhumane, and barbarous regimes. It is theUnited States which is clearly the greatest evil to peoples seeking just rights of self-determination. And it is Israel that functions as a very powerful ally and tool of the United States in this deadly insistence upon global domination. And Israel, in continued collaboration with South Africa, may yet rival and even exceed the United States in this pursuit of wrongful power. *I do not believe this is inevitable.* Suffering does not confer virtue but it does imprint a memory that, like blood, stains a life indelibly. Is it not written in Exodus, Chapter 23, Verse 9, "Ye shall not oppress a stranger, for you were strangers in the land of Egypt."

At the close of this holy week in my country, I could not avoid seeing a television ad which shows an ocean separating into two halves so that somebody could drive an Oldsmobile, a 1985

Oldsmobile, through this hideous American version of the miracle of the Red Sea. I do not believe this is inevitable or irreversible. I do not believe that we in the United States and that the people of Israel shall allow ourselves to forget and to dishonor the history of our longing for freedom. In the Old Testament it is written: *Let my people go.*

I am saying that today. I am making this appeal on behalf of First World peoples everywhere. In Exodus, it is furthermore written, "The blood shall be a sign for you." Today I am saying that our histories, the histories of Blacks and Jews in bondage and out of bondage, have been blood histories pursued through our kindred searchings for self-determination. Let this blood be a stain of honor that we share. Let us not now become enemies to ourselves and to each other.

Chapter 15

An Address to the Students of Columbia University During Their Anti-Apartheid Sit-in

April, 1985

Exactly one week ago I presented a paper on South Africa, on the connections between South Africa and the United States and between South Africa and Israel. The occasion was that of the Socialist Scholars Conference sponsored by the Democratic Socialists of America. I had been invited to participate in a South End Press-sponsored panel on Foreign Policy which included as other speakers Holly Sklar, Bogden Denitch, and Noam Chomsky. After I spoke, several people in the audience immediately attacked me: I had "hijacked the meeting" by focusing on South Africa and Israel; these countries did not warrant discussion under the heading of the U.S. Foreign Policy Panel. I had used the word holocaust "lightly." It was incorrect and unfortunate that I had thought to say, "South Africa is our holocaust." I had failed to examine events taking place in Afghanistan. And so forth. Of course many disagreed, but what depressed me most, exactly one week ago, was my feeling that so many members of the audience did not really listen to me and, therefore, so many of them did not hear what I had said.

Outside that auditorium, afterwards, a friend of mine tried to explain this not listening business by telling me that when white audiences "see somebody Black they do not hear what you actually say. They assume that they know what you think." I did not find that explanation comforting, needless to say. And I left that conference rather discouraged and rather angry. Then at the Passover Seder of some friends, that night, I heard about what you were doing, here, for the first time. I heard about your sit-ins, your fasting, your sleeping outdoors. And my entire perspective shifted with excitement and happiness. I thought that this, your anti-apartheid protests, here at Columbia, was the best possible news in a very, very long while.

The next day—or last Sunday—WBAI broadcast "The Weekend News" at 7 p.m. devoting a ten minute segment to a report on the DSA Conference. I listened to the newscaster declare that the Foreign Policy Panel had consisted of three speakers, not four. I listened to the deletion of my name, and of the subject of South Africa from the news story of that panel. This astounded me. WBAI? Not only did white audiences not really listen to a Black speaker but they would apparently take it further and erase the fact that somebody Black had spoken at all. Later WBAI broadcast my entire talk. But my experience at the conference and with WBAI's original coverage of the event left me feeling seriously bruised and threatened by these attempts to silence me.

And so I am grateful, exactly one week later, to speak with you. I want to tell you how much happiness you give, how much morale you restore, by your courageous and heroic protests here at Columbia. I want to tell you how much respect I feel and how much I admire the persevering heroism of your bravery. To me you are political heroes and political heroines coming of age despite national inertia, turpitude, and cowardice. At this moment of outstandingly senile leadership, the politics of a senile cowboy leading the ignorant into a never never land of blundering lies and unconscionable idiotic outcries such as "Say 'Uncle'!" you are young and brilliantly well-informed and centered on justice. That senile cowboy flying around in appropriate clown's makeup rightly fears the inevitable revelation of his moral and intellectual decrepitude. He rightly fears exposure of his uselessness in a world of progressive majorities of people who, by definition, neither long for death nor glorify the monstrous deficiencies of the past.

For more than two weeks you, students here at Columbia University, have dared to disturb the peace. You have dared to disrupt the order of the day. By making your anti-apartheid witness, here at Columbia University, you have dared to disturb that worthless, phony peace that does not wait on justice. You have dared to disrupt the order of the day that means unmitigated nightmare to the more than twenty-two million Africans of South Africa. Only yesterday, in the *New York Times*, (April 12, 1985)

Boyers Naude, Secretary General of the South African Council of
Churches, called for Americans to "do all they can to support the
efforts in their own country—by churches, academic institutions
and their organizations—to press their government to change its
disastrous policy toward South Africa."

Consistent with that call, you do not, you cannot, support this
particular institution, without a mighty protest. At the present time
Columbia maintains an investment of $34 million in South Africa.
At the present time, the Board of Trustees of this particular
institution refuses even to meet with you, its students, who
question this apparent collaboration with the only country on the
planet that has been universally condemned as an outlaw
nation/state, a criminal state, an illegal, boasting, bloated, racist
regime obsessively opposed to the legitimate needs of those
persecuted and starving and thirsty and moaning and weary and
terrorized Black lives inside South Africa, those lives of 72% of the
citizens of South Africa: the Africans of South Africa!

Because this particular institution, this Columbia University,
maintains not only $34 million of investment in South Africa,
because, therefore, this Columbia University also maintains what
it describes as "its right" to collaborate with the fiendish godfor-
saking system of apartheid in South Africa, you, the students of
Columbia, do not, and cannot support this institution without
protest. And neither can I, a Barnard College alumna.

Only evil will collaborate with evil. That is something you
know with your minds and with your hearts and with your bodies,
out here, hour after hour, uncertain of food, uncertain of warmth,
and openly threatened with expulsion or suspensions or criminal
arrest.

But who is talking "legal"? In the context of this university's
investment in the horrors of injustice, in the context of this
university's consequent support for the system of apartheid, in the
context of this university's substantial and greedy gambling with
the 20th century crime that is, in fact, South Africa, who is there
who may represent this university to you and presume to speak
about "the law"?

What is the law if it will sanction profit and property where it
will not first prosecute murder and theft and slavery?

And who is there, who may represent this university to you, its
students, and presume to speak of "higher education"? What could
that be?

In the context of this collaboration between Columbia University and South Africa—a collaboration as substantial and as greedy as $34 million— who shall presume to teach you something more important than the adamantine truth of your own wisdom: *Only evil will collaborate with evil.*

Halfway through this past week, I spoke with my friend, Michael Ratner at the Center for Constitutional Rights. In 1968, he was one of those arrested here at Columbia University during those historic demonstrations, and has pursued a distinguished, important career as a radical attorney and activist. I called Michael as my friend and as my legal counsel. The aftermath of my speech on the DSA's Foreign Policy Panel had become threatening, and the harrassment of misrepresentation and other things had become rather worrisome.

Michael told me I would have to decide when it was time to withdraw. "It's your body, your life, finally," he said. And then he told me how the guzanos—Cuban exiles—had sent him a wreath, threatening to kill him, earlier this year. And he had then had to decide whether to hide out for a while or just go home/go about his business, in spite of this threat. Michael Ratner, an absolute hero for justice, told me, "You have to decide: What is the limit of your courage; when that must stop."

And I thought about his loving counsel. And then I thought about you, the students of Columbia, sustaining your heroic witness against South African apartheid. And I thought yes, Michael is right. Except there is something else. And certainly he knows it: there is the question of the limit of fear, there is the question of the limit of tyranny.

And that is what you, the students of Columbia, say to all Americans as you sustain this protest: fear of reprisals stops here with my body. Tyrannical rule and tyrannical force stop here with my body.

Reprisals may come. Tyranny may continue. But tyrannical rule and tyrannical force will have to deal with me, with my body, with my open and speaking big mouth as long as I am alive.

And this heroic, this courageous action that you take here perfectly mirrors the miraculous heroism, the awesome courage of the militant revolutionary Africans of South Africa today who, in spite of their poverty, who, in spite of their absences of legal rights to assemble, to speak, to bear arms, nonetheless uphold a more and more victorious war against apartheid.

I would like to propose additional, necessary, North American acts of solidarity with the liberation struggle of Black South Africa. I would like to propose the following:

That we call in and write to support the Omnibus bill introduced by Congressman Ronald Dellums, bill HR 997, which stipulates immediate and complete disinvestment by American companies now collaborating with South Africa.

That we call in and write to support HR 1134 introduced by Congressman Charles Rangel. HR 1134 disallows tax credits for foreign investments by Americans wishing to collaborate with South Africa.

That we call in and write to support HR 1460 that prohibits new investments in South Africa and that explicitly bans computers and software sales to South Africa and that explicitly bars the import of Krugerrands from South Africa.*

And beyond this I wish to call for support—material and political—of you the students of Columbia University. I ask for phone calls and letters on your behalf, addressed to the President of this University who has had the audacity to make an atrocious attempt to prevent and misrepresent the absolutely clear and unvarying demand of Nobel Prize winner Bishop Desmond Tutu for divestment. His demand is your demand. And how should President Sovern dare to invoke Bishop Tutu's name against the righteous action of your protest here?

And beyond this I propose that we seriously cash in on the pro-life rhetoric, the freedom fighter, the contra rhetoric of the Reagan administration. Is it a good thing, is it a noble thing, is it a mandatory thing that we, the United States of America, conduct ourselves in a "pro-life" fashion? That we, the United States of America, arm and train and feed and clothe and house the "contras," the "freedom fighters?" Then let us demand of the President of our country, and let us demand of our Congresspeople, a purification of those terms. Let us demand that, finally, that, at last, we act to support, to fund, and to arm and to bolster the true pro-life forces of the world, the true freedom fighters of South Africa.

---

*As I write, July 22, 1985, immediately prior to sending this book to the press, the South African government has declared a State of Emergency which establishes total censorship of the press and total freedom for

Let us demand material aid for the African National Congress in South Africa. Who can argue against this proposal? What are the reasons why we should not purify our language, and purify our conduct as a world power, and, therefore, put our money where our mouth is: freedom? life? contra-repression? Material aid for the African National Congress in South Africa!

And, beyond this, I propose that we demand new legislation that will explicitly stipulate that any country receiving U.S. aid shall receive *no* further U.S. aid if that aid is used to constitute or to purchase arms of military cooperation with South Africa. Period.

And, finally, I congratulate you on your daring, your courage, and the heroism of your historic example, here, at Columbia University.

Truly, it seems to me, this was the moment, and this was the place, and you were the ones where the truth that only evil will collaborate with evil became a nationwide inspiration against inertia, turpitude, and cowardice. I thank you.

"security forces" arrayed against Black South African in thirty-six magisterial districts. Since September, 1984 more than 500 Black South Africans have been killed. In this morning's *New York Times*, there is this report, "Four black people were killed today, the police spokesman said, when officers opened fire with shotguns on as many as 400 demonstrators in the black township of Tumahole."

Here, in the United States, Dellums' bill has been defeated but managed to get seventy-seven votes on the floor of the House and, in view of the most recent actions by the Botha administration, its stipulations may well have a future chance of becoming incorporated into additional legislation related to South Africa. In the meantime, the Gray Bill, HR 1416 has been adopted by the House. This places five sanctions into effect:
1. No government loans to South Africa
2. No computer sales to South Africa
3. No nuclear cooperation with South Africa
4. No importation of Krugerrands into this country.
5. No new investments, including a ban on private loans.
The Senate agrees to the first three sanctions and a compromise is under negotiation between the Senate and the House with respect to sanctions number four and five.

Chapter 16

Nobody Mean More to Me Than You[1]
And the Future Life of Willie Jordan
July, 1985

Black English is not exactly a linguistic buffalo; as children, most of the thirty-five million Afro-Americans living here depend on this language for our discovery of the world. But then we approach our maturity inside a larger social body that will not support our efforts to become anything other than the clones of those who are neither our mothers nor our fathers. We begin to grow up in a house where every true mirror shows us the face of somebody who does not belong there, whose walk and whose talk will never look or sound "right," because that house was meant to shelter a family that is alien and hostile to us. As we learn our way around this environment, either we hide our original word habits, or we completely surrender our own voice, hoping to please those who will never respect anyone different from themselves: Black English is not exactly a linguistic buffalo, but we should understand its status as an endangered species, as a perishing, irreplaceable system of community intelligence, or we should expect its extinction, and, along with that, the extinguishing of much that constitutes our own proud, and singular identity.

What we casually call "English," less and less defers to England and its "gentlemen." "English" is no longer a specific matter of geography or an element of class privilege; more than thirty-three countries use this tool as a means of "intranational communication."[2] Countries as disparate as Zimbabwe and Malaysia, or Israel and Uganda, use it as their non-native currency of convenience. Obviously, this tool, this "English," cannot function inside thirty three discrete societies on the basis of rules and values absolutely determined somewhere else, in a thirty-fourth other country, for example.

123

In addition to that staggering congeries of non-native users of English, there are five countries, or 333,746,000 people, for whom this thing called "English" serves as a native tongue.[3] Approximately 10% of these native speakers of "English" are Afro-American citizens of the U.S.A. I cite these numbers and varieties of human beings dependent on "English" in order, quickly, to suggest how strange and how tenuous is any concept of "Standard English." Obviously, numerous forms of English now operate inside a natural, an uncontrollable, continuum of development. I would suppose "the standard" for English in Malaysia is not the same as "the standard" in Zimbabwe. I know that standard forms of English for Black people in this country do not copy that of whites. And, in fact, the structural differences between these two kinds of English have intensified, becoming more Black, or less white, despite the expected homogenizing effects of television[4] and other mass media.

Nonetheless, white standards of English persist, supreme and unquestioned, in these United States. Despite our multi-lingual population, and despite the deepening Black and white cleavage within that conglomerate, white standards control our official and popular judgements of verbal proficiency and correct, or incorrect, language skills, including speech. In contrast to India, where at least fourteen languages co-exist as legitimate Indian languages, in contrast to Nicaragua, where all citizens are legally entitled to formal school instruction in their regional or tribal languages, compulsory education in America compels accomodation to exclusively white forms of "English." White English, in America, is "Standard English."

This story begins two years ago. I was teaching a new course, "In Search of the Invisible Black Woman," and my rather large class seemed evenly divided between young Black women and men. Five or six white students also sat in attendance. With unexpected speed and enthusiasm we had moved through historical narratives of the 19th century to literature by and about Black women, in the 20th. I had assigned the first forty pages of Alice Walker's *The Color Purple*, and I came, eagerly, to class that morning:

"So!" I exclaimed, aloud. "What did you think? How did you like it?"

The students studied their hands, or the floor. There was no response. The tense, resistant feeling in the room fairly astounded me.

At last, one student, a young woman still not meeting my eyes, muttered something in my direction:

"What did you say?" I prompted her.

"Why she have them talk so funny. It don't sound right."

"You mean the language?"

Another student lifted his head: "It don't look right, neither. I couldn't hardly read it."

At this, several students dumped on the book. Just about unanimously, their criticisms targeted the language. I listened to what they wanted to say and silently marvelled at the similarities between their casual speech patterns and Alice Walker's written version of Black English.

But I decided against pointing to these identical traits of syntax; I wanted not to make them self-conscious about their own spoken language—not while they clearly felt it was "wrong." Instead I decided to swallow my astonishment. Here was a negative Black reaction to a prize winning accomplishment of Black literature that white readers across the country had selected as a best seller. Black rejection was aimed at the one irreducibly Black element of Walker's work: the language—Celie's Black English. I wrote the opening lines of *The Color Purple* on the blackboard and asked the students to help me translate these sentences into Standard English:

You better not never tell nobody but God. It'd kill your mammy.

Dear God,

    I am fourteen years old. I have always been a good girl. Maybe you can give me a sign letting me know what is happening to me.

    Last spring after Little Lucious come I heard them fussing. He was pulling on her arm. She say it too soon, Fonso. I aint well. Finally he leave her alone. A week go by, he pulling on her arm again. She say, Naw, I ain't gonna. Can't you see I'm already half dead, an all of the children.[5]

Our process of translation exploded with hilarity and even hysterical, shocked laughter: The Black writer, Alice Walker, knew what she was doing! If rudimentary criteria for good fiction includes the manipulation of language so that the syntax and diction of sentences will tell you the identity of speakers, the probable age and sex and class of speakers, and even the locale—urban/rural/southern/western—then Walker had written, perfectly. This is the translation into Standard English that our class produced:

> *Absolutely, one should never confide in anybody besides God. Your secrets could prove devastating to your mother."*

Dear God,

I am fourteen years old. I have always been good. But now, could you help me to understand what is happening to me?

Last spring, after my little brother, Lucious, was born, I heard my parents fighting. My father kept pulling at my mother's arm. But she told him, "It's too soon for sex, Alfonso. I am still not feeling well." Finally, my father left here alone. A week went by, and then he began bothering my mother, again: Pulling her arm. She told him, "No, I won't! Can't you see I'm already exhausted from all of these children?"

(Our favorite line was "It's too soon for sex, Alphonso.")

Once we could stop laughing, once we could stop our exponentially wild improvisations on the theme of Translated Black English, the students pushed me to explain their own negative first reactions to their spoken language on the printed page. I thought it was probably akin to the shock of seeing yourself in a photograph for the first time. Most of the students had never before seen a written facsimile of the way they talk. None of the students had ever learned how to read and write their own verbal system of communication: Black English. Alternatively, this fact began to baffle or else bemuse and then infuriate my students. Why not? Was it too late? Could they learn how to do it, now? And, ultimately, the final test question, the one testing my sincerity: Could I teach them? Because I had never taught anyone Black English and, as far as I knew, no one, anywhere in the United States, had ever offered such a course, the best I could say was "I'll try."

He looked like a wrestler.

He sat dead center in the packed room and, every time our eyes met, he quickly nodded his head as though anxious to reassure, and encourage, me.

Short, with strikingly broad shoulders and long arms, he spoke with a surprisingly high, soft voice that matched the soft bright movement of his eyes. His name was Willie Jordan. He would have seemed even more unlikely in the context of Contemporary Women's Poetry, except that ten or twelve other Black men were taking the course, as well. Still, Willie was conspicuous. His extreme fitness, the muscular density of his presence underscored the riveted, gentle attention that he gave to anything anyone said. Generally, he did not join the loud and rowdy dialogue flying back and forth, but there could be no doubt about his interest in our discussions. And, when he stood to present an argument he'd prepared, overnight, that nervous smile of his vanished and an irregular stammering replaced it, as he spoke with visceral sincerity, word by word.

That was how I met Willie Jordan. It was in between "In Search of the Invisible Black Women" and "The Art of Black English." I was waiting for Departmental approval and I supposed that Willie might be, so to speak, killing time until he, too, could study Black English. But Willie really did want to explore Contemporary Women's poetry and, to that end, volunteered for extra research and never missed a class.

Towards the end of that semester, Willie approached me for an independent study project on South Africa. It would commence the next semester. I thought Willie's writing needed the kind of improvement only intense practice will yield. I knew his intelligence was outstanding. But he'd wholeheartedly opted for "Standard English" at a rather late age, and the results were stilted and frequently polysyllabic, simply for the sake of having more syllables. Willie's unnatural formality of language seemed to me consistent with the formality of his research into South African apartheid. As he projected his studies, he would have little time, indeed, for newspapers. Instead, more than 90% of his research would mean saturation in strictly historical, if not archival, material. I was certainly interested. It would be tricky to guide him into a more confident and spontaneous relationship both with language and apartheid. It was going to be wonderful to see what happened when he could catch up with himself, entirely, and talk back to the world.

September, 1984: Breezy fall weather and much excitment! My class, "The Art of Black English," was full to the limit of the fire laws. And, in Independent Study, Willie Jordan showed up, weekly, fifteen minutes early for each of our sessions. I was pretty happy to be teaching, altogether!

I remember an early class when a young brother, replete with his ever present pork-pie hat, raised his hand and then told us that most of what he'd heard was "all right" except it was "too clean." "The brothers on the street," he continued, "they mix it up more. Like 'fuck' and 'motherfuck.' Or like 'shit.'" He waited. I waited. Then all of us laughed a good while, and we got into a brawl about "correct" and "realistic" Black English that led to Rule 1.

Rule 1: *Black English is about a whole lot more than mothafuckin.*

As a criterion, we decided, "realistic" could take you anywhere you want to go. Artful places. Angry places. Eloquent and sweetalkin places. Polemical places. Church. And the local Bar & Grill. We were checking out a language, not a mood or a scene or one guy's forgettable mouthing off.

It was hard. For most of the students, learning Black English required a fallback to patterns and rhythms of speech that many of their parents had beaten out of them. I mean *beaten*. And, in a majority of cases, correct Black English could be achieved only by striving for *incorrect* Standard English, something they were still pushing at, quite uncertainly. This state of affairs led to Rule 2.

Rule 2: *If it's wrong in Standard English it's probably right in Black English, or, at least, you're hot.*

It was hard. Roommates and family members ridiculed their studies, or remained incredulous, "You *studying* that shit? At school?" But we were beginning to feel the companionship of pioneers. And we decided that we needed another rule that would establish each one of us as equally important to our success. This was Rule 3.

Rule 3: *If it don't sound like something that come out somebody mouth then it don't sound right. If it don't sound right then it ain't hardly right. Period.*

This rule produced two weeks of compositions in which the students agonizingly tried to spell the sound of the Black English sentence they wanted to convey. But Black English is, pre-eminently, an oral/spoken means of communication. *And spelling don't talk.* So we needed Rule 4.

Rule 4: *Forget about the spelling. Let the syntax carry you.*

Once we arrived at Rule 4 we started to fly because syntax, the structure of an idea, leads you to the world view of the speaker and reveals her values. The syntax of a sentence equals the structure of your consciousness. If we insisted that the language of Black English adheres to a distinctive Black syntax, then we were postulating a profound difference between white and Black people, *per se*. Was it a difference to prize or to obliterate?

There are three qualities of Black English—the presence of life, voice, and clarity—that testify to a distinctive Black value system that we became excited about and self-consciously tried to maintain.

1. Black English has been produced by a pre-technocratic, if not anti-technological, culture. More, our culture has been constantly threatened by annihilation or, at least, the swallowed blurring of assimilation. Therefore, our language is a system constructed by people constantly needing to insist that we exist, that we are present. Our language devolves from a culture that abhors all abstraction, or anything tending to obscure or delete the fact of the human being who is here and now/the truth of the person who is speaking or listening. Consequently, *there is no passive voice construction possible in Black English.* For example, you cannot say, "Black English is being eliminated." You must say, instead, "White people eliminating Black English." The assumption of the presence of life governs all of Black English. Therefore, overwhelmingly, *all action takes place in the language of the present indicative.* And every sentence assumes the living and active participation of at least two human beings, the speaker and the listener.

2. A primary consequence of the person-centered values of Black English is the delivery of voice. If you speak or write Black English, your ideas will necessarily possess that otherwise elusive attribute, *voice.*

3. One main benefit following from the person-centered values of Black English is that of *clarity.* If your idea, your sentence, assumes the presence of at least two living and active people, you will make it understandable because the motivation behind every sentence is the wish to say something real to somebody real.

As the weeks piled up, translation from Standard English into Black English or vice versa occupied a hefty part of our course work.

Standard English (hereafter S.E.): "In considering the idea of studying Black English those questioned suggested—"

(What's the subject? Where's the person? Is anybody alive in there, in that idea?)

Black English (hereafter B.E.): "I been asking people

> what you think about somebody studying Black English
> and they answer me like this:"

But there were interesting limits. You cannot "translate" instances of Standard English preoccupied with abstraction or with nothing/nobody evidently alive, into Black English. That would warp the language into uses antithetical to the guiding perspective of its community of users. Rather you must first change those Standard English sentences, themselves, into ideas consistent with the person-centered assumptions of Black English.

Guidelines For Black English

1. Minimal number of words for every idea: This is the source for the aphoristic and/or poetic force of the language; eliminate every possible word.

2. Clarity: If the sentence is not clear it's not Black English.

3. Eliminate use of the verb *to be* whenever possible. This leads to the deployment of more descriptive and therefore, more precise verbs.

4. Use *be* or *been* only when you want to describe a chronic, ongoing state of things.

> He *be* at the office, by 9. (He is always at the office by 9.)
> He *been* with her since forever.

5. Zero copula: Always eliminate the verb *to be* whenever it would combine with another verb, in Standard English.

> S.E.: She is going out with him.
> B.E.: She going out with him.

6. Eliminate *do* as in:

> S.E.: What do you think? What do you want?
> B.E.: What you think? What you want?

Rules number 3, 4, 5, and 6 provide for the use of the minimal number of verbs per idea and, therefore, greater accuracy in the choice of verb.

7. In general, if you wish to say something really positive, try to formulate the idea using emphatic negative structure.

> S.E.: He's fabulous.
> B.E.: He bad.

8. Use double or triple negatives for dramatic emphasis.

S.E.: Tina Turner sings out of this world.
B.E.: Ain nobody sing like Tina.

9. Never use the *-ed* suffix to indicate the past tense of a verb.

S.E.: She closed the door.
B.E.: She close the door. Or, she have close the door.

10. Regardless of intentional verb time, only use the third person singular, present indicative, for use of the verb *to have*, as an auxiliary.

S.E.: He had his wallet then he lost it.
B.E.: He have him wallet then he lose it.
S.E.: He had seen that movie.
B.E.: We seen that movie. Or, we have see that movie.

11. Observe a minimal inflection of verbs. Particularly, never change from the first person singular forms to the third person singular.

S.E. Present Tense Forms: He goes to the store.
B.E.: He go to the store.
S.E.: Past Tense Forms: He went to the store.
B.E.: He go to the store. Or, he gone to the store. Or, he been to the store.

12. The possessive case scarcely ever appears in Black English. Never use an apostrophe ('s) construction. If you wander into a possessive case component of an idea, then keep logically consistent: *ours, his, theirs, mines.* But, most likely, if you bump into such a component, you have wandered outside the underlying world-view of Black English.

S.E.: He will take their car tomorrow.
B.E.: He taking they car tomorrow.

13. Plurality: Logical consistency, continued: If the modifier indicates plurality then the noun remains in the singular case.

S.E.: He ate twelve doughnuts.
B.E.: He eat twelve doughnut.
S.E.: She has many books.
B.E.: She have many book.

14. Listen for, or invent, special Black English forms of the past tense, such as: "He losted it. That what she felted." If they are clear and readily understood, then use them.

Do not hesitate to play with words, sometimes inventing them: e.g. "astropotomous" means huge like a hippo plus astronomical and, therefore, signifies real big.

16. In Black English, unless you keenly want to underscore the past tense nature of an action, stay in the present tense and rely on the overall context of your ideas for the conveyance of time and sequence.

17. Never use the suffix -*ly* form of an adverb in Black English.

    S.E.: The rain came down rather quickly.

    B.E.: The rain come down pretty quick.

18. Never use the indefinite article *an* in Black English.

    S.E.: He wanted to ride an elephant.

    B.E.: He want to ride him a elephant.

19. Invarient syntax: in correct Black English it is possible to formulate an imperative, an interogative, and a simple declarative idea with the same syntax:

    B.E.: You going to the store?

        You going to the store.

        You going to the store!

Where was Willie Jordan? We'd reached the mid-term of the semester. Students had formulated Black English guidelines, by consensus, and they were now writing with remarkable beauty, purpose, and enjoyment:

    I ain hardly speakin for everybody but myself so under-stan that."—Kim Parks

Samples from student writings:

    "Janie have a great big ole hole inside her. Tea Cake the only thing that fit that hole...

    "That pear tree beautiful to Janie, especial when bees fiddlin with the blossomin pear there growin large and lovely. But personal speakin, the love she get from starin at that tree ain the love what starin back at her in them relationship." (Monica Morris)

    "Love is a big theme in, *They Eye Was Watching God*. Love show people new corners inside theyself. It pull out good stuff and stuff back bad stuff...Joe worship the doing uh his own hand and need other people to worship him too. But he ain't think about

Janie that she a person and ought to live like anybody common do. Queen life not for Janie." (Monica Morris)

"In both life and writin, Black womens have varietous experience of love that be cold like a iceberg or fiery like a inferno. Passion got for the other partner involve, man or woman, seem as shallow, ankle-deep water or the most profoundest abyss." (Constance Evans)

"Family love another bond that ain't never break under no pressure." (Constance Evans)

"You know it really cold/When the friend you/Always get out the fire/Act like they don't know you/When you in the heat." (Constance Evans)

"Big classroom discussion bout love at this time. I never take no class where us have any long arguin for and against for two or three day. New to me and great. I find the class time talkin a million time more interestin than detail bout the book." (Kathy Esseks)

As these examples suggest, Black English no longer limited the students, in any way. In fact, one of them, Philip Garfield, would shortly "translate" a pivotal scene from Ibsen's *Doll House*, as his final term paper:

> Nora: I didn't gived no shit. I thinked you a asshole back then, too, you make it so hard for me save mines husband life.
> Krogstad: Girl, it clear you ain't any idea what you done. You done exact what once done, and I losed my reputation over it.
> Nora: You asks me believe you once act brave save you wife life?
> Krogstad: Law care less why you done it.
> Nora: Law must suck.
> Krogstad: Suck or no, if I wants, judge screw you wid dis paper.
> Nora: No way, man. (Philip Garfield)

But where was Willie? Compulsively punctual, and always thoroughly prepared with neatly typed compositions, he had disappeared. He failed to show up for our regularly scheduled conference, and I received neither a note nor a phone call of explanation. A whole week went by. I wondered if Willie had finally been captured by the extremely current happenings in

South Africa: passage of a new constitution that did not enfranchise the Black majority, and militant Black South African reaction to that affront. I wondered if he'd been hurt, somewhere. I wondered if the serious workload of weekly readings and writings had overwhelmed him and changed his mind about independent study. Where was Willie Jordan?

One week after the first conference that Willie missed, he called: "Hello, Professor Jordan? This is Willie. I'm sorry I wasn't there last week. But something has come up and I'm pretty upset. I'm sorry but I really can't deal right now."

I asked Willie to drop by my office and just let me see that he was okay. He agreed to do that. When I saw him I knew something hideous had happened. Something had hurt him and scared him to the marrow. He was all agitated and stammering and terse and incoherent. At last, his sadly jumbled account let me surmise, as follows: Brooklyn police had murdered his unarmed, twenty-five year old brother, Reggie Jordan. Neither Willie nor his elderly parents knew what to do about it. Nobody from the press was interested. His folks had no money. Police ran his family around and around, to no point. And Reggie was really dead. And Willie wanted to fight, but he felt helpless.

With Willie's permission I began to try to secure legal counsel for the Jordan family. Unfortunately Black victims of police violence are truly numerous while the resources available to prosecute their killers are truly scarce. A friend of mine at the Center for Constitutional Rights estimated that just the preparatory costs for bringing the cops into court normally approaches $180,000. Unless the execution of Reggie Jordan became a major community cause for organizing, and protest, his murder would simply become a statistical item.

Again, with Willie's permission, I contacted every newspaper and media person I could think of. But the Wiliam Bastone feature article in *The Village Voice* was the only result from that canvassing.

Again, with Willie's permission, I presented the case to my class in Black English. We had talked about the politics of language. We had talked about love and sex and child abuse and and men and women. But the murder of Reggie Jordan broke like a hurricane across the room.

There are few "issues" as endemic to Black life as police violence. Most of the students knew and respected and liked Jordan. Many of them came from the very neighborhood where the murder had occurred. All of the students had known somebody close to them who had been killed by police, or had known frightening moments of gratuitous confrontation with the cops. They wanted to do everything at once to avenge death. Number One: They decided to compose personal stamedia person I could think of. But the William Bastons feature tements of condolence to Willie Jordan and his family, written in Black English. Number Two: They decided to compose individual messages to the police, in Black English. These should be prefaced by an explanatory paragraph composed by the entire group. Number Three: These individual messages, with their lead paragraph, should be sent to *Newsday*.

The morning after we agreed on these objectives, one of the young women students appeared with an unidentified visitor, who sat through the class, smiling in a peculiar, comfortable way.

Now we had to make more tactical decisions. Because we wanted the messages published, and because we thought it imperative that our outrage be known by the police, the tactical question was this: Should the opening, group paragraph be written in Black English or Standard English?

I have seldom been privy to a discussion with so much heart at the dead heat of it. I will never forget the eloquence, the sudden haltings of speech, the fierce struggle against tears, the furious throwaway, and useless explosions that this question elicited.

That one question contained several others, each of them extraordinarily painful to even contemplate. How best to serve the memory of Reggie Jordan? Should we use the language of the killers—Standard English—in order to make our ideas acceptable to those controlling the killers? But wouldn't what we had to say be rejected, summarily, if we said it in our own language, the language of the victim, Reggie Jordan? But if we sought to express ourselves by abandoning our language wouldn't that mean our suicide on top of Reggie's murder? But if we expressed ourselves in our own language wouldn't that be suicidal to the wish to communicate with those who, evidently, did not give a damn about us/Reggie/police violence in the Black community?

At the end of one of the longest, most difficult hours of my own life, the students voted, unanimously, to preface their individual

messages with a paragraph composed in the language of Reggie
Jordan. *"At least we don't give up nothing else. At least we stick to
the truth: Be who we been. And stay all the way with Reggie."*

It was heartbreaking to proceed, from that point. Everyone in
the room realized that our decision in favor of Black English had
doomed our writings, even as the distinctive reality of our Black
lives always has doomed our efforts to "be who we been" in this
country.

I went to the blackboard and took down this paragraph,
dictated by the class:

"...YOU COPS!
WE THE BROTHER AND SISTER OF WILLIE JORDAN,
A FELLOW STONY BROOK STUDENT WHO THE BRO-
THER OF THE DEAD REGGIE JORDAN. REGGIE, LIKE
MANY BROTHER AND SISTER, HE A VICTIM OF BRUTAL
RACIST POLICE, OCTOBER 25, 1984. US APPALL, FED UP,
BECAUSE THAT ANOTHER SENSELESS DEATH WHAT
OCCUR IN OUR COMMUNITY. THIS WHAT WE FEEL,
THIS, FROM OUR HEART, FOR WE AIN'T STAYIN' SILENT
NO MORE:"

With the completion of this intrduction, nobody said anything. I asked for comments. At this invitation, the unidentified
visitor, a young Black man, ceaselessly smiling, raised his hand.
He was, it so happens, a rookie cop. He had just joined the force in
September and, he said, he thought he should clarify a few things.
So he came forward and sprawled easily into a posture of bar-
room, or fireside, nostalgia:

"See," Officer Charles enlightened us, "Most times when you
out on the street and something come down you do one of two
things. Over-react or under-react. Now, if you under-react then you
can get yourself kilt. And if you over-react then maybe you kill
somebody. Fortunately it's about nine times out of ten and you will
over-react. So the brother got kilt. And I'm sorry about that,
believe me. But what you have to understand is what kilt him:
Over-reaction. That's all. Now you talk about Black people and
white police but see, now, I'm a cop myself. And (big smile) I'm
Black. And just a couple months ago I was on the other side. But
see it's the same for me. You a cop, you the ultimate authority: the
Ultimate Authority. And you on the street, most of the time you
can only do one of two things: over-react or under-react. That's all

it is with the brother: Over-reaction. Didn't have nothing to do
with race."

That morning Officer Charles had the good fortune to escape
without being boiled alive. But barely. And I remember the pride of
his smile when I read about the fate of Black policemen and other
collaborators, in South Africa. I remember him, and I remember
the shock and palpable feeling of shame that filled the room. It
was as though that foolish, and deadly, young man had just
relieved himself of his foolish, and deadly, explanation, face to
face with the grief of Reggie Jordan's father and Reggie Jordan's
mother. Class ended quietly. I copied the paragraph from the
blackboard, collected the individual messages and left to type
them up.

Newsday rejected the piece.

The Village Voice could not find room in their "Letters"
section to print the individual messages from the students to the
police.

None of the tv news reporters picked up the story.

Nobody raised $180,000 to prosecute the murder of Reggie
Jordan.

Reggie Jordan is really dead.

I asked Willie Jordan to write an essay pulling together
everything important to him from that semester. He was still
deeply beside himself with frustration and amazement and loss.
This is what he wrote, un-edited, and in its entirety:

"Throughout the course of this semester I have been researching the effects of oppression and exploitation along racial
lines in South Africa and its neighboring countries. I have become
aware of South African police brutalization of native Africans
beyond the extent of the law, even though the laws themselves are
catalyst affliction upon Black men, women and children. Many
Africans die each year as a result of the deliberate use of police
force to protect the white power structure.

"Social control agents in South Africa, such as policemen, are
also used to force compliance among citizens through both overt
and covert tactics. It is not uncommon to find bold-faced coercion
and cold-blooded killings of Blacks by South African police for
undetermined and/or inadequate reasons. Perhaps the truth is
that the only reasons for this heinous treatment of Blacks rests in
racial differences. We should also understand that what is con-

veyed through the media is not always accurate and may sometimes be construed as the tip of the iceberg at best.

"I recently received a painful reminder that racism, poverty, and the abuse of power are global problems which are by no means unique to South Africa. On October 25, 1984 at approximately 3:00 p.m. my brother, Mr. Reginald Jordan, was shot and killed by two New York City policemen from the 75th precinct in the East New York section of Brooklyn. His life ended at the age of twenty-five. Even up to this current point in time the Police Department has failed to provide my family, which consists of five brothers, eight sisters, and two parents, with a plausible reason for Reggie's death. Out of the many stories that were given to my family by the Police Department, not one of them seems to hold water. In fact, I honestly believe that the Police Department's assessment of my brother's murder is nothing short of ABSOLUTE BULLSHIT, and thus far no evidence had been produced to alter perception of the situation.

Furthermore, I believe that one of three cases may have occurred in this incident. First, Reggie's death may have been the desired outcome of the police officer's action, in which case the killing was premeditated. Or, it was a case of mistaken identity, which clarifies the fact that the two officers who killed my brother and their commanding parties are all grossly incompetent. Or, both of the above cases are correct, i.e., Reggie's murderers intended to kill him and the Police Department behaved insubordinately.

Part of the argument of the officers who shot Reggie was that he had attacked one of them and took his gun. This was their major claim. They also said that only one of them had actually shot Reggie. The facts, however, speak for themselves. According to the Death Certificate and autopsy report, Reggie was shot eight times from point-blank range. The Doctor who performed the autopsy told me himself that two bullets entered the side of my brother's head, four bullets were sprayed into his back, and two bullets struck him in the back of the his legs. It is obvious that unnecessary force was used by the police and that it is extremely difficult to shoot someone in his back when he is attacking or approaching you.

After experiencing a situation like this and researching South Africa I believe that to a large degree, justice may only exist as rhetoric. I find it difficult to talk of true justice when the oppression of my people both at home and abroad attests to the fact that inequality and injustice are serious problems whereby Blacks and Third World people are perpetually short-changed by society. Something has to be done about the way in which this world is set up. Although it is a difficult task, we do have the power to make a change."

—Willie J. Jordan Jr.
EGL 487, Section 58, November 14, 1984

It is my privilege to dedicate this book to the future life of Willie J. Jordan Jr.
August 8, 1985

Chapter 17

White Tuesday
November, 1984

Whole campaign an' dint neither one of them joker talk about right or wrong. We knowed it was trouble.

'Mos anytime you see whitemen spose to be fight each other an' you not white well you know you got trouble because they blah-blah loud about Democrat or Republican an' they huffin' an puff about democracy someplace else but relentless, see, the deal come down evil on somebody don' have no shirt an' tie, somebody don' live in no whiteman house no whiteman country.

Anyway they ain' never say boo about right or wrong.

Number One lie all the time. He smile a lot. An' look like Number Two he hope to die before he call a lie a lie. He smile a little bit himself.

Now Number One love him some camera. Seem like the camera mean freedom from the bother of the truth. Number One tell astropotamous story about how him unilateral disarm an' how him never no way attack them program for the poor an' how him dedicate to real people right to life an' that why everybody (Everybody) better off, on camera, right? The womens an 'the children an' the Spanish-speakin' an' the oldfolk an' the trees don' grow no more because we better off.

Number Two he go *uh-huh uh-huh but-but uh-huh uh-huh but-but uh-huh*

But everybody better off an' Lebanon a wonderland.

Nuclear missiles store inside the New York City harbor an'.the carrier "Intrepid" float because that boat so big and ugly it jus' scare the enemy to death.

You an' me the enemy.

Number One done sit that saddle for a long long time an' he don' never get confuse. He straightshoot at them Indian like a cowboy. He recognize a Indian when he see one.

Indian proliferate like Communist. Indian gone gay. Indian don' pray, (in school). Indian pow-wow in Moscow. Indian dance The Grenada. Indian under water. Indian upside the sky. Indian ship cheeseburger into El Salvador. Indian make heap big mess in whiteman backyard do not tolerate no fence.

(I have ast a Indian.)

Meanwhile Number Two he go eeny eeny myney mo oh me oh my oh maybe this horse or maybe that horse or maybe he forget about what horse an' walk him wobbly kinda walk that leave them Indian in puzzlement.

We knowed it was trouble.

Growed up whitemen getaway with murder.

Number One tell about the difference between Nicaragua an' El Salvador like night an' day. He say El Salvador horror like the sunshine next to Nicaragua have no light bulb have no helicopter have no hospital no Uncle Sam jam guns and F-15s an' more an' more marine into the outdoor kitchen of the hungry. Number Two say zip

Number Two say zip

Number Two say Castro Dictate Che Guevara Contemptible an' Jesse Jackson Independent.

Number One say zip

Number One say zip

Number One tell astropotamous story about apartheid an' South Africa. He say constructive somethin'. He say progress somehow. He say listen close now how the U.S.A. ain' no asylum for no freedom fighters lessen they on the payroll. He not studyin' no justice. He say nothin' about blood.

Number Two he only say South Africa what hurt him nice guy image.

Number One say zip.

Whole campaign an' don' neither one of them joker talk about right or wrong.

But then we vote.

We push down for Number Two because we figure well at least he not predictable. And because at least him wife know how she get the body outtabed without she landin' on she head.

We vote.

Whole campaign an' dint neither one of them joker talk about right or wrong. We knowed it was trouble.

We been livin' with trouble for awhile.

An' we still here.

We still right here.

Chapter 18

Moving Beyond the Enemy
Israel and South Africa
August, 1985

During the first half of this year, the American left has spent itself trying to stop things. Fourteen million dollars to the contras had to be stopped. New bank loans to South Africa had to be stopped. CIA management of "humanitarian aid" to the contras had to be stopped. Importation of South African kruggerrands had to be stopped. We have exhausted ourselves in strictly defensive maneuvers. This has made sense since the peoples we hope to assist are neither aggressive nor offensive. In Nicaragua, the people want to defend the democratic sovereignty that they fought for. In South Africa, the people want to defend themselves from the atrocity of apartheid and to achieve the sovereignty that universal human rights confer.

Perhaps the most important contribution we can make to international justice is just this: Stop United States' collaboration with the enemies of self-determination. This will keep us busy. This will run us ragged. This may make the difference that so many millions of First World peoples live for: The difference between freedom and death.

As the Reagan administration jostles its propaganda against Nicaragua, as its aircraft carriers and its mercenary soldiers lock into place and as the Reagan administration throttles economic assistance to Nicaragua, as it blocks deliveries of laundry soap and penicillin and toilet paper and measles' vaccine, the choice for the Sandinistas daily simplifies into nothing more than freedom or death. In South Africa, the Botha regime has declared a State of Emergency, now in its eighth day. That is the white point of view. In the eyes of Black people, South Africa has meant a state of

145

emergency—debasement and terror and exploitation and intolerable infant and adult mortality rates—since the imposition, by force, of racist minority rule. In the context of "the State of Emergency" it is ludicrous to speak of "the taking away of rights" from Black people. What rights? The right to boil water? The right to mine somebody else's diamonds? The right to clean somebody else's house?

As the concept of rights is commonly understood, the majority of the people of South Africa have no rights, but one: the right to die as they choose to die. That is what we are witnessing, now, as we watch the steady uprisings of an otherwise powerless multitude. It is the invincible Black exercise of this last and only unassailable human right, the right to die—to challenge the bullets, unarmed, to mock the almighty, unarmed, to transform a funeral into an outcry, a revolt, against death. The alternative to freedom in South Africa is the living death of apartheid.

As I write, it seems likely that the Congress will deepen its complicity with Reagan's obsessional wish to overthrow the duly elected government of Nicaragua. Bit by bit enfeeblement of Congressional resistance to Reagan's peristaltic reflex against that small, poor country will require resilient patch and clip efforts just to give one more Nicaraguan mother a month in which she can learn how to read, or one more Nicaraguan father a week to help finish the re-building of a clinic blown up by the contras.

As I write, it seems likely that the Congress will move a few millimeters away from the inertia, "the constructive engagement" with apartheid that the Reagan administration boasts about. By the end of the summer, a compromise bill will probably ooze out of the House and the Senate, establishing minor league, beginner sanctions. But even such pitiful increments of respectable activity are not guaranteed. Passage of these belated sanctions into law will depend upon the indefatigable prodding forward of those anti-heroes, our legislators. And then we will need to remind them, our elected representatives, that they have simply begun, not finished, their work against this evil. We will have to insist that the amazing tumult of South Africa is not "a tragedy," as the *New York Times* (July 28, 1985), has declared, but rather the first episodes of a war in which there exist, as usual, two sides. How will we, the United States, altogether oppose the wrong side? How will we, the United States, altogether support the right side? With this perspective, we must summon up further, aggressively militant legislation against apartheid.

But defense is, by definition, a limited undertaking.

No matter how beleaguered their days have been, the people of Nicaragua have always made room in their lives for the preservation of a vision of what they positively, passionately hope to create: the ways that they hope to share the farming of the land, the responsibility for production, the administration of schools, the political representation of their numerous political parties. And they have taken the offensive against malaria and dysentery and villages without electricity, or roads.

No matter how difficult, the majority Black peoples of South Africa have cultivated a concept of dignity and a vision of a non-racist egalitarian society that propels them again and again, to defy the awesome military force of apartheid with no shoes on their feet, and nowhere to run.

Can we presume to do less? Do we have less time and fewer resources than the Sandinistas?

I believe that the American left has become intimidated by right-wing rhetoric laying claims to the flag and all that the flag flies above. Instead, we could usefully imitate those we hope to assist:

As we oppose aid to the contras, let us also propose massive foreign aid to the Sandinista government.

As we oppose investment in South Africa, let us also propose massive foreign aid to the frontline states of Angola and Mozambique.

As Director of the Southern Africa Project, Gay McDougall recently told me, "Equal in importance to the all important sanctions against South Africa is the shoring up of the frontline States—Angola, Mozambique and Lesothu—that will abet the development of model independent African nations that can stand up to a hostile South Africa and still feed their people. This is where U.S. foreign aid becomes indispensable. If they feel they can stand up to South Africa and yet not starve, then these frontline countries will be able to afford to provide humanitarian assistance, or whatever kind of assistance they choose, to the A.N.C., for example, and still survive. The war (in South Africa) can neither be waged nor won without rear bases of operation for the revolutionaries."

I believe that we, on the American left, can become at least as bold as the pro-lifers who say they would arm freedom fighters and protect democracy, around the world. As the allies of all movements for self-determination, we need to renew our own claims to the flag—to our rightful powers of representation, and we need to assert our own pro-life policies as pro-life, identify our own freedom fighters, and stipulate our own conditions for the furtherance of democracy. There is much more that we must do, besides attempting to checkmate the enemy. Let us, at last, emulate the astonishing and aggressive faith of the majority peoples of the world.

Where are we and whose country is this anyway?

Addendum

WHAT YOU CAN DO ABOUT NICARAGUA

Stay informed. Call or write to the following:

*Center for Constitutional Rights (offers a booklet on two lawsuits filed by U.S. Representative Ronald V. Dellums against the Reagan administration's illegal Nicaragua policies.) 853 Broadway, 14th floor, New York, NY 10003, (212) 674-3304.

*Central American Historical Institute (publishes weekly newsletter and monthly reports), Intercultural Center, Georgetown University, Washington, D.C. 20057, (202) 625-8246.

*Coalition for a New Foreign and Military Policy (operates a 24-hour message hotline giving updates on legislation affecting Central America), (202) 483-3391.

*Congressional Black Caucus and your own state representatives and senators, in care of U.S. House of Representatives, Washington, D.C. 20515, or U.S. Senate, Washington, D.C. 20510, (202) 224-3121 (central switchboard).

*National Network in Solidarity with the Nicaraguan People, 2025 I Street N.W., Suite 402, Washington, D.C. 20006, (202) 223-2328.

*North American Congress on Latin America (offers list of films and resources), 151 West 19th Street, New York, NY 10011, (212) 989-8890.

Notes

For the Sake of a People's Poetry

1. from "I Sing the Body Electric," by Walt Whitman
2. from Section XII of *The Heights of Macchu Picchu,* translated by Nathaniel Tarn, Farrar Straus and Giroux: New York.
3. from *The Heights of Macchu Picchu,* translated by Ben Bolitt, Evergreen Press.
4. from "Woes and the Furies," by Pablo Neruda in *Selected Poems of Neruda,* translated by Ben Bolitt, p. 10⁻
5. Ibid. "The Dictators," p. 161
6. from "Song of Myself" by Walt Whitman
7. from "There was a Child Went Forth" by Walt Whitman
8. from "Crossing Brooklyn Ferry"
9. from "Song of Myself"
10. from "Song of the Rolling Earth"

Black Folks on Nicaragua

1. 11/30/82 press release issued by U.S. Congressman Ronald Dellums, on the occasion of his signing on as a plaintiff in the case, *Sanchez v. Reagan.*
2. This is a direct quote of remarks made by the attorney Michael Ratner during a telephone conversation in July, 1983.
3. Ibid.
4. This is quoted from a telephone conversation that I held with U.S. Congressman Major Owens in July, 1983.
5. This is quoted from a telephone conversation that I held with U.S. Congressman Mickey Leland in July, 1983.

Life After Lebanon

1.In 1984, Geraldine Ferraro became the first woman candidate for vice-president in the United States.

2. In 1984, inordinate pressure was put upon Jesse Jackson to "repudiate" remarks by Minister Louis Farrakhan. Although Farrakhan quite mirrors Jesse Hems and Jerry Falwell in his hatefulness and extremities of view, Farrakhan does not possess a fraction of the power and the following that both Helms and Falwell can actually claim.

3. Jesse Jackson's address to the Democratic Convention. August, 1985.

The Blood Shall be a Sign Unto You

1. *Exodus*, Chapter 12, Verse 13

2. Chomsky, Noam, *The Fateful Triangle,* p. 7, footnote 11, *Time,* 10/11/82. Chomsky adds, "Israelis tend to rank their power one notch higher, describing themselves as the third most powerful military force in the world."

3. Ibid., p. 11.

4. *In These Times*, May 22, 1985, "Released apartheid foe attacks Israel's ties to South Africa," by Beit-Hallahmi.

5. Ibid.

6. Ibid.

7. Ibid.

8. *New Outlook,* March-April, 1983, "Israel and South Africa 1977-1982: Business as usual—and more," by Benjamin Beit-Hallahmi.

9. The London *Sunday Times*, 4/15/84, "The Unnatural Alliance," by John Adams

10. Ibid.

11. In 1974, The General Assembly of the United Nations condemned the collaboration between South Africa and Israel as an "unholy alliance."

12. *The Jerusalem Post*, "Twinning with a Tyrant," 11/9/84, by Roy Iscowitz.

13. *New York Times,* 1/6/83, "Israel's Global Ambitions," by Benjamin Beit Hallahmi

Nobody Mean More to Me Than You

1. Black English aphorism crafted by Monica Morris, a Junior at S.U.N.Y. at Stony Brook, October, 1984.

2. *English is Spreading, But What Is English.* A presentation by Professor S.N. Sridahr, Dept. of Linguistics, S.U.N.Y. at Stonybrook, April 9, 1985: Dean's Conversation Among the Disciplines.

3. Ibid.

4. *New York Times*, March 15, 1985, Section One, p 14: Report on study by Linguistics at the University of Pennsylvania.

5. Alice Walker, *The Color Purple,* p. 11, Harcourt Brace, N.Y.

About the Author

The political writer June Jordan is a leading poet of international acclaim. To date she has published sixteen books and her poems, articles, essays, and reviews appear frequently in publications nationwide.

Represented in numerous anthologies, she is a member of the Board of Directors for Poets and Writers, Inc. and the Center for Constitutional Rights.

In addition to her many political activities, she has taught at CCNY, Sarah Lawrence College, and Yale University. Currently, she is a professor of English at SUNY Stonybrook.

In 1969, Jordan received a Rockefeller grant in creative writing. In 1970, she received the Prix de Rome in environmental design. In 1972, her novel *His Own Where* was a finalist for the National Book Award. In 1976, she was Reed Lecturer at Barnard College. In 1978, she received a C.A.P.S. grant and in 1982 she received an NEA fellowship. In 1985 she won a New York Foundation for the Arts Fellowship in poetry and a Massachusetts Council for the Arts award for her essay, "On the Difficult Miracle of Black Poetry, Or Something Like a Sonnet for Phillis Wheatley," included here.

Civil Wars, her previous collection of political essays was the first such work to be published by a Black woman in the United States. *On Call* is her second volume of political writings.